Scottish Borders Street

CW00694553

CONTE?

Area of Coverage	2-3	Ke	7
Berwick-upon-Tweed	4-7	Langholm & Lauder	28-29
Canonbie & Chirnside	8-9	Lockerbie	30-31
Coldingham, Coldstream &	10-11	Melrose	32-33
Cornhill-on-Tweed		Moffat & Newcastleton	34-35
Duns & Earlston	12-13	Newton St Boswells & St Boswells	36-37
Eyemouth & Gordon	14-15	Peebles	38-39
Galashiels	16-19	Selkirk & St Abbs	40-41
Greenlaw & Hawick	20-23	Walkerburn & Index to Walkerburn,	42-44
Innerleithen & Jedburgh	24-25	Berwick-upon-Tweed & Galashiels	

KEY TO MAP SYMBOLS

A74(M) — Motorway	● ● ● ● Antonine wall (course of)
A1 — Primary route dual / single	P F Parking / filling station
A698 — A road dual / single	PO L Post office / library
B6461 — B road dual / single	H S Hospital / superstore
Unclassified road	B i Bus station / tourist information centre
Pedestrian street	▣ a Castle / antiquity
Track / path	⊞ ✳ Historic house / garden
Town wall	m ⚘ Museum / viewpoint
Long distance footpath	▲ ⬠ Camping / caravan site
Railway and station	★ ✝ Other tourist attraction / church
National border	Woodland / recreation or cemetery
● ● ● Police / fire / ambulance station	Built-up area / water
◆ ◆ Coastguard / lifeboat station	Shingle / sand
▲ ▼ △ Primary / secondary / special school	Rocks / mud

Scale 1:14 000

0 —————— 500m

0 —————— 500yds

ISBN 978 1 86097 227 6

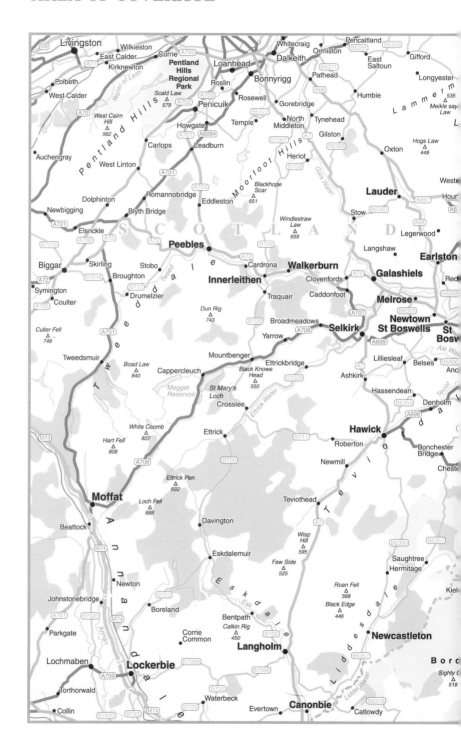

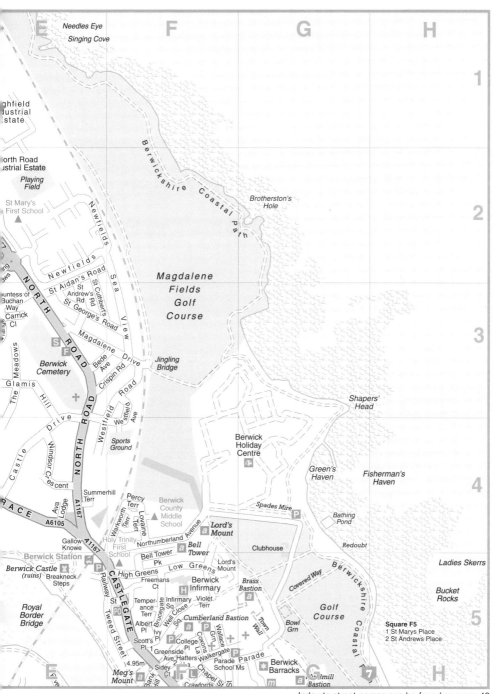

E — Needles Eye / Singing Cove

F

G

H

ghfield
ustrial
state

orth Road
ustrial Estate

Playing Field

St Mary's First School

Berwickshire Coastal Path

Brotherston's Hole

1

2

untess of Buchan Way

Carrick Cl

Newfields

Newfields

St Aidan's Road

St Andrew's Rd

St Cuthberts Rd

St George's Road

Sea View

NORTH ROAD

Magdalene Drive

Bede Ave

Crispin Rd

Westfield Road

Westfield Ave

Magdalene Fields Golf Course

Jingling Bridge

Shapers' Head

3

The Meadows

Glamis

Castle Hill Drive

Windsor Crescent

Ave Lodge

Sports Ground

Berwick Cemetery

Berwick Holiday Centre

Green's Haven

Fisherman's Haven

4

ACE

A6105

A1167

Summerhill Terr

Percy Terr

Warkworth Terr

Lovaine Terr

Berwick County Middle School

Northumberland Avenue

Spades Mire

Bathing Pond

Redoubt

Lord's Mount

Bell Tower

Clubhouse

Berwick Station

Gallow Knowe

Holy Trinity First School

Bell Tower Pk

Lord's Mount

Covered Way

Berwickshire Coastal Path

Ladies Skerrs

5

Berwick Castle (ruins)

Breakneck Steps

Royal Border Bridge

CASTLEGATE

Railway St

Tweed Street

High Greens

Freemans Ct

Temperance Terr

Albert Pl

Scott's Pl

Ivy Pl

Low Greens

Brucegate

Well Close

Sidey Ct

College Pl

Greenside Ave

Hatters La

Bank

Chapel St

Meg's Mount

Berwick Infirmary

Violet Terr

Infirmary Sq

Wallace Grn

Coxons La

Parade

Parade

Walkergate

Cumberland Bastion

Brass Bastion

Town Wall

Bowl Grn

Golf Course

Bucket Rocks

Berwick Barracks

Imill Bastion

Berwick School Ms

4.95m

Crawfords St

Square F5
1 St Marys Place
2 St Andrews Place

7

H

Index to street names can be found on page 42

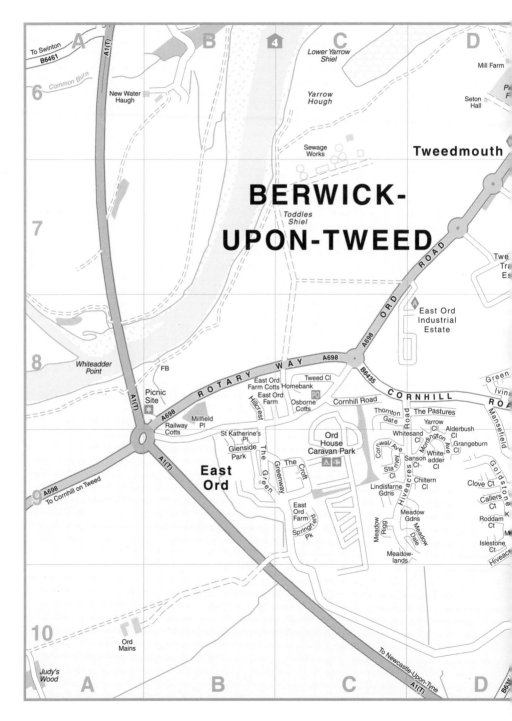

BERWICK-UPON-TWEED

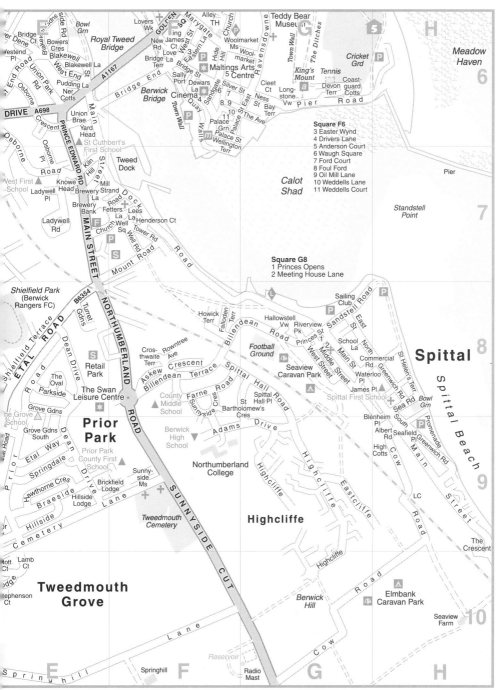

Square F6
3 Easter Wynd
4 Drivers Lane
5 Anderson Court
6 Waugh Square
7 Ford Court
8 Foul Ford
9 Oil Mill Lane
10 Weddells Lane
11 Weddells Court

Square G8
1 Princes Opens
2 Meeting House Lane

Index to street names can be found on page 42

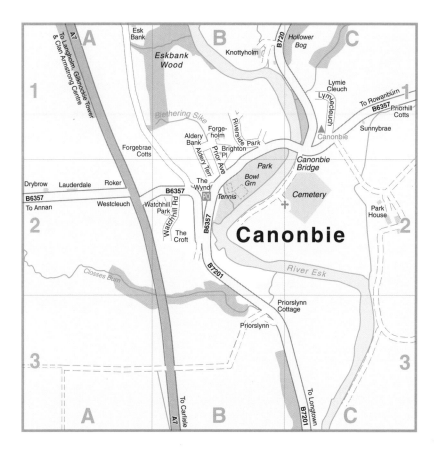

Index to Canonbie

Aldery Bank   B1
Aldery Terrace   B2
Brighton Place   B1
Forgebrae Cottages   A1
Forgeholm   B1
Lymiecleuch   C1
Prior Avenue   B1
Priorhill Cottages   C1
Riverside Park   B1
Watchhill Park   B2
Watchhill Road   B2
Wynd, The   B2

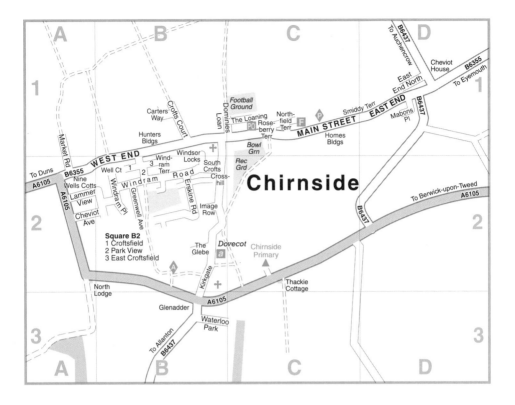

Index to Chirnside

Carters Way	B1	Image Row	B2	Well Court	B2
Cheviot Avenue	A2	Kirkgate	B2	West End	A2
Crofts Court	B1	Lammer View	A2	Windram Place	B2
Croftsfield (1)	B2	Loaning, The	C1	Windram Road	B2
Crosshill	B2	Mabons Place	D1	Windram Terrace	B2
Dominies Loan	B1	Main Street	C1	Windsor Locks	B1
East Croftsfield (3)	B2	Market Road	A1		
East End	D1	Nine Wells Cottages	A2		
East End North	D1	Northfield Terrace	C1		
Erskine Road	B2	Park View (2)	B2		
Glebe, The	B2	Roseberry Terrace	C1		
Greenwell Avenue	B2	Smiddy Terrace	C1		
Homes Buildings	C1	South Crofts	B2		
Hunters Buildings	B1	Waterloo Park	B3		

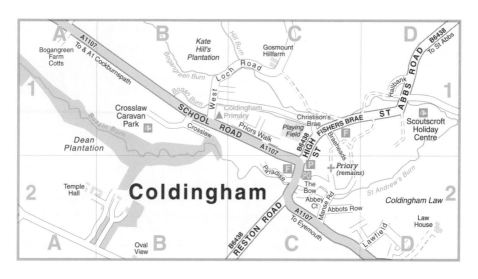

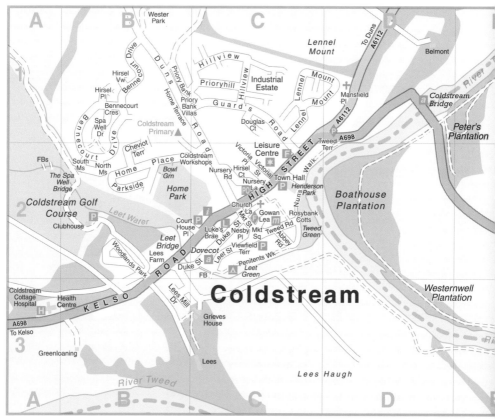

Index to Coldingham

Abbey Court	C2
Abbots Row	C2
Bogangreen Farm Cottages	A1
Bow, The	C2
Braeheads	C1
Christison's Brae	C1
Crosslaw	B1
Fishers Brae	C1
Hallbank	D1
High Street	C1
Lawfield	D2
Manse Road	C2
Paradise	C2
Priorswalk	C1
Reston Road	C2
St Abbs Road	D1
School Road	B1
West Loch Road	B1

Index to Coldstream & Cornhill on Tweed

Abbey Road	C2
Bennecourt Crescent	B1
Bennecourt Drive	B1
Cheviot Terrace	B2
Court House Place	B2
Church Lane	C2
Douglas Court	C1
Duke Street	B2, C2
Duns Road	B1
Gowan Lea	C2
Green Lane	G2
Guard's Road	C1
High Street	C2
Hillview	C1
Hirsel Court	C2
Hirsel Place	B1
Hirsel View	B1
Home Place	B2
Home Terrace	B1
Kelso Road	B3
Knowehead	F3
Lees Mill Drive	B3
Leet Street	C2
Lennel Mount	C1
Luke's Brae	C2
Main Street	F3
Mansfield Place	D1
Market Square	C2
Market Street	C2
Milestone Cottages	F3
Nesby Place	C2
North Mews	B2
Nuns Walk	C2
Nursery Lane	C2
Nursery Road	C2
Parkside	B2
Penitents Walk	C2
Priory Bank	B1
Priory Bank Villas	B1
Prioryhill	C1
Rosybank Cottages	C2
St Helens Gardens	F3
Sidings, The	G2
South Mews	B2
Spa Well Drive	B1
Station Cottages	G2
Station Gardens	G3
Tweed Road	C2
Tweed Terrace	C1
Victoria Place	C2
Victoria Street	C2
Viewfield Terrace	C2
Woodlands Park	B2

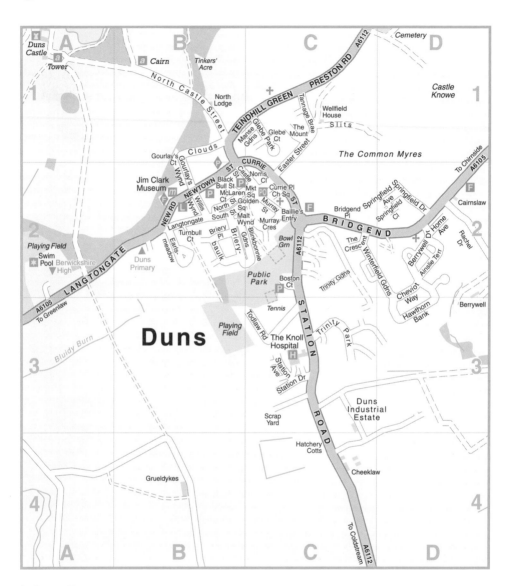

Index to Duns

Ainslie Terrace	D2	Briery Place	B2	Currie Street	C2	Hatchery	C4
Bailie's Entry	C2	Brierybaulk	B2	Earlsmeadow	B2	Cottages	
Berrywell Drive	D2	Castle Street	B2	Easter Street	C2	Hawthorn Bank	D3
Black Bull Street	B2	Cheviot Way	D2	Glebe Court	C1	Home Avenue	D2
Blinkbonnie Gardens	C2	Church Square	C2	Glebe Park	C1	Langtongate	A3, B2
Boston Court	C2	Clouds	B1	Golden Square	B2	McLaren Court	B2
Bridgend	C2	Crescent, The	C2	Gourlay's Court	B1	Malt Wynd	B2
Bridgend Place	C2	Currie Place	C2	Gourlay's Wynd	B1	Manse Gardens	C1

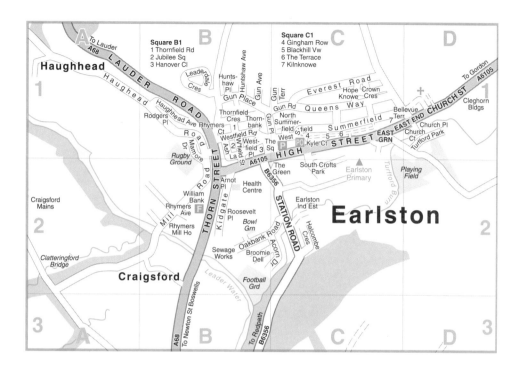

Market Square	C2	Turnbull Court	B2	Gingham Row (4)	C1	Oakbank Road	B2
Mount, The	C1	Willis Wynd	B2	Green, The	C2	Queens Way	C1
Murray Crescent	C2	Winterfield Gardens	C2	Gun Avenue	B1	Rhymer's Court	B1
Murray Street	C2			Gun Place	B1	Rhymers Avenue	B2
New Road	B2			Gun Road	C1	Roosevelt Place	B2
Newtown Street	B2			Gun Terrace	C1	Rodgers Place	B1
Norris Close	C2			Halcombe Crescent	C2	South Crofts Park	C2
North Castle Street	B1	**Index to Earlston**		Hanover Close (3)	B1	Square, The	B1
North Street	B2			Haughhead Avenue	B1	Station Road	C2
Preston Road	C1			Haughhead Road	A1	Summerfield	C1
Rachel Drive	D2	Acorn Drive	C2	High Street	C1	Terrace, The (6)	C1
Slits	C1	Arnot Place	B2	Hope Knowe	C1	Thorn Street	B2
Springfield Avenue	D2	Ash Lane	B1	Huntshaw Avenue	B1	Thornbank	B1
Springfield Close	D2	Bellevue Terrace	C1	Huntshaw Place	B1	Thornfield Crescent	B1
Springfield Drive	D2	Blackhill View (5)	C1	Jubilee Square (2)	B1	Thornfield Road (1)	B1
South Street	B2	Broomie Dell	B2	Kidgate	B2	Turfford Park	D1
Station Avenue	C3	Church Court	D1	Kilnknowe (7)	C1	West Summerfield	C1
Station Drive	C3	Church Place	D1	Kyle Court	C2	Westfield Place	B1
Station Road	C3	Church Street	D1	Lauder Road	B1	Westfield Road	B1
Tannage Brae	C1	Cleghorn Buildings	D1	Leaderdale	B1	Westfield Street	B1
Teindhill Green	B1	Crown Crescent	C1	Crescent		William Bank	B2
Todlaw Road	C3	East End	C1	Mamore Drive	B1		
Trinity Gardens	C2	East Green	C1	Mill Road	B2		
Trinity Park	C3	Everest Road	C1	North Summerfield	C1		

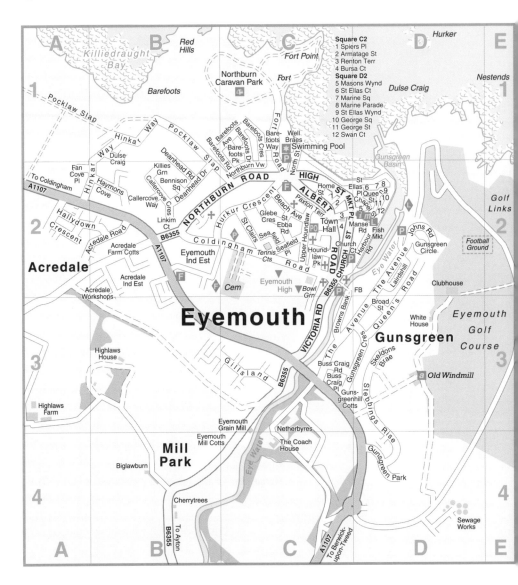

Index to Eyemouth

Acredale Road	A2	Barefoots Crescent	C1
Albert Road	C2	Barefoots Drive	C1
Armatage	C2	Barefoots Park	C1
Street (2)		Barefoots Road	B1
Avenue, The	C3	Barefoots Way	C1
Avenue, The	D2	Beach Avenue	C2
Barefoots Avenue	C1	Bennison Square	B2

Broad Street	D3	Callercove Way	B2
Browns Bank	C3	Chapel Street	D2
Bursa Court (4)	C2	Church Street	C2
Buss Craig Place	C3	Coldingham Road	C2
Buss Craig Road	C3	Deanhead Drive	B2
Callercove	B2	Deanhead Road	B1
Crescent		Dulse Craig	B1

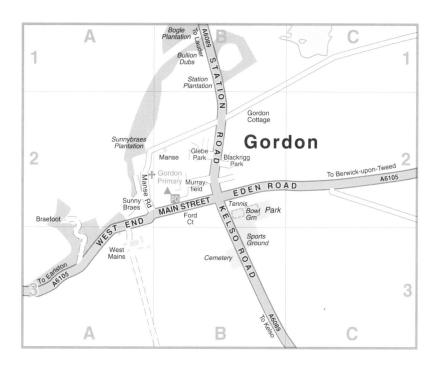

Eyemouth Mill Cottages	C4	Hurkur Crescent	B2	Seafield Place	C2
Fan Cove Place	A2	Johns Road	D2	Skeldons Brae	D3
Fort Road	C1	Killies Green	B2	Spiers Place (1)	C2
George Square (10)	D2	Lairds Hill	D2	Stebbings Rise	D3
		Linkim Court	B2	Swan Court (12)	D2
George Street (11)	D2	Manse Road	D2	Upper Houndlaw	C2
		Marine Parade (8)	D2	Victoria Road	C3
Gillsland	C3	Marine Square (7)	D2	Well Braes	C1
Glebe Crescent	C2	Market Place	C2		
Gunsgreen Circle	D2	Masons Wynd (5)	D2		
Gunsgreen Crescent	C3	North Street	C2		
		Northburn Road	B2	**Index to Gordon**	
Gunsgreen Park	D4	Northburn View	C2		
Gunsgreenhill Cottages	C3	Paxton Terrace	C2	Blackrigg Park	B2
		Pocklaw Slap	A1	Eden Road	B2
Hallydown Crescent	A2	Queen Street	D2	Ford Court	B2
		Queen's Road	D3	Glebe Park	B2
Harbour Road	D2	Renton Terrace (3)	C2	Kelso Road	B2
Haymons Cove	B2	St Clairs	C2	Main Street	B2
High Street	C2	St Ebba Road	C2	Manse Road	A2
Hinkar Way	A2, B1	St Ellas Place	D2	Murrayfield	B2
Home Street	C2	St Ellas Wynd (9)	D2	Station Road	B2
Houndlaw Park	C2	Seafield	C2	Sunny Braes	A2
				West End	A3

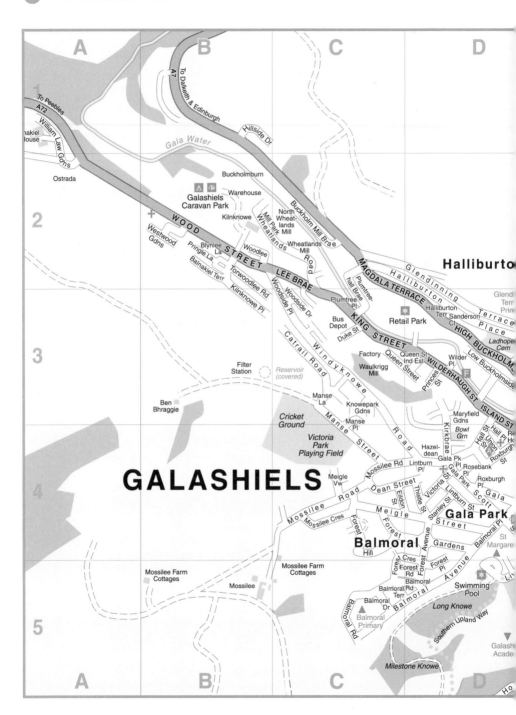

GALASHIELS

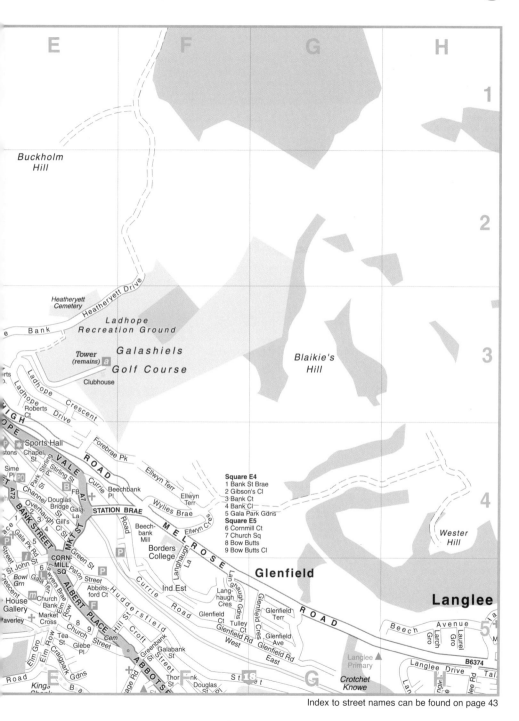

E
F
G
H

1

2

3

4

5

Buckholm
Hill

Heatheryett
Cemetery

Heatheryett Drive

Bank

Ladhope
Recreation Ground

Galashiels

Tower
(remains)

Golf Course

Clubhouse

Blaikie's
Hill

Ladhope Crescent

Roberts
Ct

HIGH

Ladhope
Drive

HOPE

Sports Hall

stons Chapel
St

Sime
Pl PO

A72

Stirling St

Channel

Park St

Douglas
Bridge

Overhaugh
St

Gill's
Ct

BANK STREET

Gala Pk Rd

Vale
Road

Currie

FB

Gala
La

Forebrae Pk

Beechbank
Pl

STATION BRAE

MKT ST

Green St

Ellwyn Terr

Ellwyn
Terr

Wylies Brae

Ellwyn Cres

MELROSE

Beech-
bank
Mill

Road

Square E4
1 Bank St Brae
2 Gibson's Cl
3 Bank Ct
4 Bank Cl
5 Gala Park Gdns
Square E5
6 Cornmill Ct
7 Church Sq
8 Bow Butts
9 Bow Butts Cl

Wester
Hill

Street

John
St

Bowl
Grn

Gala Terr

CORN
MILL
SQ

Paton
Street

Hill St

ALBERT PLACE

Abbots-
ford Ct

Borders
College

Ind Est

Langhaugh La

Currie

Road

ROAD

Glenfield

Langlee

House
Gallery

averley

Church
Bank

Market
Cross

Church
Street

Glebe
Pl

Huddersfield

Croft

Greenbank
St

Galabank
St

Lang-
haugh
Cres

Glenfield
Ct

Glenfield

Glenfield
West

Langhaugh Gdns

Tulley
Ct

Glenfield Rd

Glenfield Cres

Glenfield
Terr

Glenfield
Ave

Glenfield Rd
East

Beech

Avenue

Larch
Gro

Laurel
Gro

Gro

B6374

Elm Gro

Elm Row

Tea

Craigpark
Gdns

ABBOTS

Road

Kings

B

a

Thor
St

nk

St

Douglas
St

18

Langlee
Primary

Crotchet
Knowe

Langlee Drive

Tal

Index to street names can be found on page 43

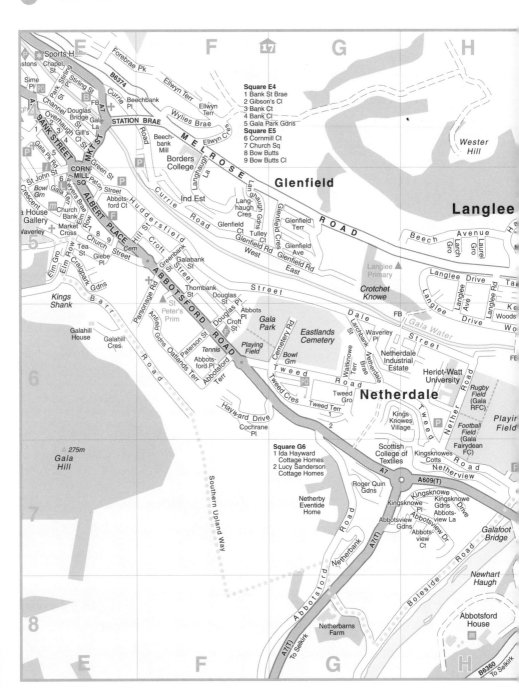

Square E4
1 Bank St Brae
2 Gibson's Cl
3 Bank Ct
4 Bank Cl
5 Gala Park Gdns
Square E5
6 Cornmill Ct
7 Church Sq
8 Bow Butts
9 Bow Butts Cl

Glenfield

Langlee

Netherdale

Square G6
1 Ida Hayward
Cottage Homes
2 Lucy Sanderson
Cottage Homes

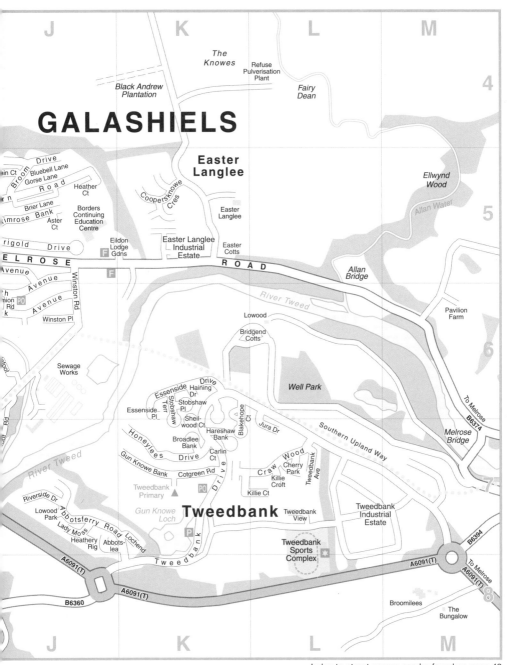

GALASHIELS

The Knowes

Refuse Pulverisation Plant

Black Andrew Plantation

Fairy Dean

Drive
in Ct
Broom
Bluebell Lane
Gorse Lane
R o a d
Heather Ct
n
Brier Lane
imrose Bank
Aster Ct
Borders Continuing Education Centre

Easter Langlee

Cooperskowe Cres

Easter Langlee

Ellwynd Wood

Allan Water

rigold Drive
Eildon Lodge Gdns F
Easter Langlee Industrial Estate
Easter Cotts

E L R O S E
Avenue
Avenue
h
nion Rd PO
k
Avenue
Winston Rd
Winston Pl

R O A D F

Allan Bridge

River Tweed

Lowood

Bridgend Cotts

Sewage Works

Essenside
Haining Dr
Drive
Stobshaw Pl
Stobshaw Terr
Sheilwood Ct
Essenside Pl
Blakehope Ct
Jura Dr

Well Park

To Melrose
B6374

Southern Upland Way

Melrose Bridge

Pavilion Farm

Honeylees
Broadlee Bank
Hareshaw Bank
Carlin Ct
Wood
Craw
Cherry Park
Killie Croft
Tweedbank Ave

Rd
River Tweed
Gun Knowe Bank
Cotgreen Rd
Drive
Killie Ct

Riverside Dr
Lowood Park
Abbotsferry Road
Lady Moss
Heathery Rig
Abbotslea
Lochend

Tweedbank Primary PO

Gun Knowe Loch

Tweedbank

P

Tweedbank
Tweedbank View

Tweedbank Industrial Estate

B6394

A6091(T)
B6360
A6091(T)
Tweedbank
Tweedbank Sports Complex

A6091(T)
To Melrose
A6091(T)

Broomilees
The Bungalow

Index to street names can be found on page 43

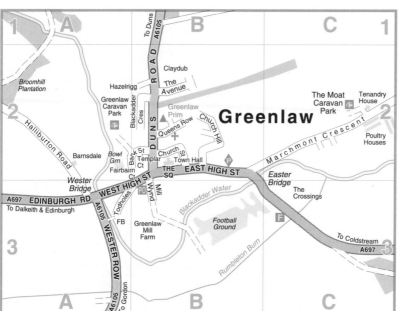

Index to Greenlaw

Avenue, The	B2
Bank Street	B2
Blackadder Crescent	B2
Church Hill	B2
Church Street	B2
Duns Road	B2
East High Street	B2
Edinburgh Road	A3
Fairbairn Court	B2
Halliburton Road	A2
Marchmont Crescent	C2
Mill Wynd	B3
Queens Row	B2
Square, The	B2
Templar Court	B2
Todholes	A3
West High Street	A3
Wester Row	A3

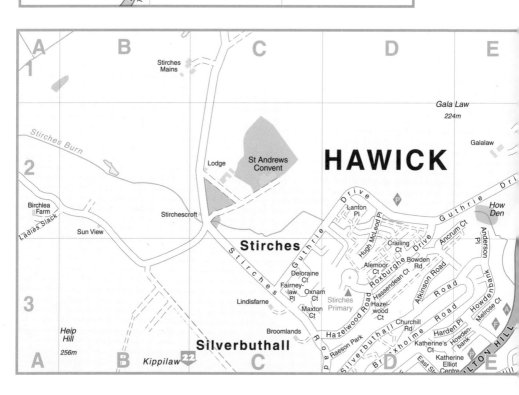

Index to Hawick

Albert Road	22 D5	Bourtree Bank	22 D5	Cavers View	21 G2	Douglas Haig	23 E5	Henderson	21 F2
		Bourtree Place	22 D5	Charles Street	21 F2	Court (2)		Road	

Albert Road 22 D5
Alemoor Court 20 D3
Allars Bank 22 D6
Allars Crescent 22 D6
Ancrum Court 20 D2
Anderson Place 20 E3
Appletreehall 21 F2
  Road
Arthur Street 22 E4
Atkinson Road 20 D3
Backdam Gate 22 D6
Bailleul Grove 23 F5
Baker Street 22 D5
Bath Street 22 D5
Beaconsfield 22 C6
  Terrace
Beaconsfield 22 C6
  Terrace Lane (2)
Beattie Court 21 F3
Birch Cottages 23 F4
Boonraw Road 21 F2
Borthaugh 22 B6
  Road
Borthwick Court 21 F2
Borthwick Road 21 F2
Bothwell Court 22 C4

Bourtree Bank 22 D5
Bourtree Place 22 D5
Bourtree 22 E5
  Terrace (1)
Bowden Road 20 D3
Braid Road 22 E6
Branxholme 20 D3
  Road
Bright Street 22 C6
Brougham 22 D5
  Place
Bruce Court 22 C4
Buccleuch 22 C6
  Place (1)
Buccleuch 22 B7
  Road
Buccleuch 22 C6
  Street
Buccleuch 22 C6
  Terrace
Burnflat Drive 22 B7
Burnflat Lane 22 B7
Burnfoot Road 21 G2
Burnfoot Road 21 E3
Burnhead Road 21 G2
Burns Road 21 G2
Carnarvon 22 C5
  Street

Cavers View 21 G2
Charles Street 21 F2
Chay Blyth 21 F3
  Place
Cheviot Road 22 C6
Church Lane 21 E2
Churchill Road 20 D3
Commercial 22 D5
  Road
Corn Mill Court 22 D6
Crailing Court 20 D3
Croft Road 22 D5
Cross Wynd 22 B5
Crown Close (8) 22 D6
Crumhaugh 22 B7
  Hill
Crumhaugh 22 C7
  Hill Road
Crumhaugh 22 C6
  Road
Dakers Place 23 E5
Dalkeith Place 23 E5
Daykin's Drive 21 G3
Dean Road 22 B5
Deanfield Court 22 C5
Deloraine Court 20 C3
Dickson Court 22 D4
Dickson Street 22 D4

Douglas Haig 23 E5
  Court (2)
Douglas Road 23 E5
Douglas Road 23 E4
  East (4)
Dovecot Mews 22 D4
Dovecote Street 22 D4
Dovemount 22 D4
  Place
Drumlanrig 22 D6
  Court
Drumlanrig 22 C6
  Place
Drumlanrig 22 D6
  Square
Duke Street 22 E4
Earl Street 22 E4
East Stewart 20 D3
  Place
Eastfield Road 23 E4
Edina Place 22 E5
Eildon Road 21 F2
Elm Court 22 E6
Elm Grove 22 E6
Ettrick Terrace 22 E5
Fairhurst Drive 21 G3
Fairneylaw 20 C3
  Place
Fenwick Park 23 F4
Fisher Avenue 22 E6
Frank Place (10) 22 D6
Frank Scott 22 C6
  Court
Fraser Avenue 21 F2
Galalaw Road 21 F2
Garfield Street 22 D6
Gladstone 22 C6
  Street
Glebemill Street 23 E4
Glebe Place 22 E6
Green Lane 22 C6
Green Terrace 22 C6
Greenheads 22 C6
  Terrace
Greenside Hall 22 C4
  Road
Guthrie Drive 20 C3
Guthrie Drive 20 D2
Haggis Ha'brae 22 B8
Hamilton Road 21 G3
Harden Place 20 D3
Hassendean 20 D3
  Court
Havelock Place 22 D4
Havelock 22 D4
  Street
Hazelwood 20 D3
  Court
Hazelwood 20 D3
  Road

Henderson 21 F2
  Road
Heronhill Bank 23 G4
Heronhill 23 G4
  Crescent
High Street 22 D5
Hillend Drive 21 E2
Howdenbank 20 E3
Howe Gate 22 D6
Howlands 22 C5
  Terrace
Hugh McLeod 20 D3
  Place
Hunter Terrace 22 D4
Ivanhoe Terrace 21 E3
Katherine's 20 D3
  Court
Kenilworth 21 F2
  Avenue
Kirk Wynd 22 D6
Kirkstile (4) 22 D6
Ladies Slack 20 A3
Laidlaw Terrace 22 D4
Laing Terrace 22 D4
Langheugh 22 B6
  Road
Langlands Bank 22 C5
Langlands 22 C5
  Court
Langlands 22 C5
  Road
Lanton Place 20 D2
Leaburn Drive 23 F4
Leaburn Grove 23 F5
Leishman Place 21 F2
Leyden Bank 23 F4
Liddesdale 22 C8
  Crescent
Liddesdale Road 22 C7
Linden Crescent 22 E5
Linden Terrace 22 E5
Loan 22 C6
Loch Park Road 22 E5
Lockhart Place 22 E5
Lockiesedge 22 D4
Longbaulk Road 22 B7
Longcroft 22 C6
  Crescent
Longcroft Road 22 C6
Longhope Drive 22 B7
Lothian Street 22 D5
Lovel Court (7) 22 D6
McLagan Drive 21 F3
McLaren Court 21 F3
Mansfield 22 E4
  Crescent
Mansfield 23 E4
  Gardens
Mansfield Mills 22 E4
  House

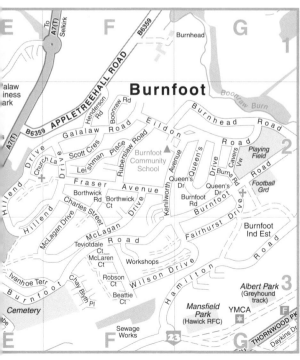

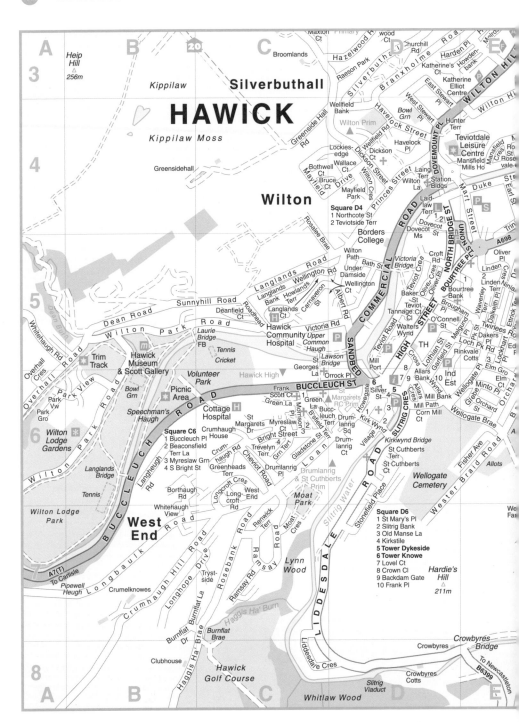

Map of Hawick showing the following labelled features:

Grid references (top): A, B, C, D, E across columns; 3, 4, 5, 6, 8 down rows.

HAWICK

Heip Hill △ 256m

Kippilaw

Silverbuthall

Kippilaw Moss

Greensidehall

Greensidehall

Wilton

Square D4
1 Northcote St
2 Teviotside Terr

Maxton Ct
Broomlands
Hazelwood Ct
wood Ct
Raeson Park
Churchill Rd
Harden Pl
Howden-bank
Katherine's Ct
Katherine Elliot Centre
WILTON HILL
Wilton Hi

Wellfield Bank
West Stewart Pl
Bowl Grn
Hunter Terr
Greenside Hall
Havelock Street
Wilton Prim
Wellfield Rd
Dickson Ct
Havelock Pl
Teviotdale Leisure Centre
Mansfield Mills Ho
Mansfield Ro
Rose vale
Lockies-edge
Bothwell Ct
Wallace Ct
Dickson Street
Wilton Cres
Bruce Ct
Drive
Laing Terr
Wilton La
Station Bldgs
Duke St
Earl St
Mayfield
Mayfield Park

Rosalee Brae
Borders College
Laid-law Terr
Dovecot St
Dovecot Ms
P S

Langlands Road
Wilton Path
Under Damside
Bath St
Wellington Ct
Victoria Bridge
Croft Rd
Oliver Pl
Linden
Langlands Bank
Wellington Rd
Howlands Terr
Langlands Rd
Carnaveron St
Albert Rd
Baker Ct
Teviot Cres
Oliver Cres
Bourtree Bank
Linden Terr
Ninia

Sunnyhill Road
Roadhead
Deanfield Ct
Langlands Ct
H
Victoria Rd
Teviot St
Tannage Cl
Brougham
O'Connell St
Waverley Terr
Dalkeith Terr
Eittrick St

Dean Road
Wilton Park Road
Laurie Bridge
FB
Tennis Cricket
Hawick Community Hospital
Upper Common Haugh
Walters Wynd
Melgund
Loch Pk
Dakers
Loch Pk Rd
Twirlees Rd
Lockhart Ed

Whitehaugh Rd
Overhall Cres
Park View
Trim Track
Hawick Museum & Scott Gallery
Volunteer Park
Hawick High
St Georges La
Lawson Bridge
Mill Port
Orrock Pl
Cross
Lothian St
Carfield St
Rinkvale Cotts
Elm Gro
Elm

Overhall Cres
Park Vw
Park Gro
Bowl Grn
Picnic Area
Speechman's Haugh
Crumhaugh House
Frank Scott Ct
Green La
Green La
Morrison Pl
St Margarets RC Prim
Buccleuch Terr
Drum-lanrig Sq
Silver St
Mill Bank
Mill Path
Corn Mill Ct
Allars Bank
Ind Est
Minto Ct
Glebe
Orchard
Wellogate Brae

Square C6
1 Buccleuch Pl
2 Beaconsfield Terr La
3 Myreslaw Grn
4 S Bright St

BUCCLEUCH ROAD
Cottage Hospital
St Margarets Dr
Bright Street
Trevelyn Terr
Gladstone Terr
Drum-lanrig Ct
Kirkwynd Bridge
St Cuthberts Terr
St Cuthberts Ct
Fisher Ave
Wester Braid Road
Allots

Wilton Lodge Gardens
Crumhaugh Rd
Crum-haugh Rd
Greenheads Terr
Myreslaw Ct
Drumlanrig Pl
Drumlanrig & St Cuthberts Prim
Loan
Wellogate Cemetery

Langlands Bridge
Tennis
Borthaugh Rd
Longcroft Cres
West End
Whitehaugh View
Long-croft Rd
Renwick Terr
Moat Park
Wellogate

Wilton Lodge Park
West End
Stonefield Place

Square D6
1 St Mary's Pl
2 Slitrig Bank
3 Old Manse La
4 Kirkstile
5 **Tower Dykeside**
6 **Tower Knowe**
7 Lovel Ct
8 Crown Cl
9 Backdam Gate
10 Frank Pl

A7(T) To Carlisle
Pipewell Heugh
Crumelknowes
Crumhaugh Hill Road
Longbaulk Road
Longhope Drive
Burnflat La
Tryst-side
Rosebank Road
Ramsay Road
Ramsay Rd
Lynn Wood
LIDDESDALE ROAD
Slitrig Water
Hardie's Hill △ 211m

Haggis Ha' Road
Burnflat Dr
Burnflat Brae
Haggis Ha' Burn
Clubhouse
Hawick Golf Course
Whitlaw Wood
Slitrig Viaduct
Liddesdale Cres
Crowbyres
Crowbyres Cotts
Crowbyres Bridge
To Newcastleton
B6399
We Fa

Doon Burn
Slitrig Water
COMMERCIAL ROAD
SANDBED
HIGH STREET
SLITRIG CRES
NORTH BRIDGE ST
BOURTREE PL
DOVEMOUNT PL
Princes Street
Mayfield Drive
Branxholme
East Stewart Pl
Mart Street
A698
Oliver Pl

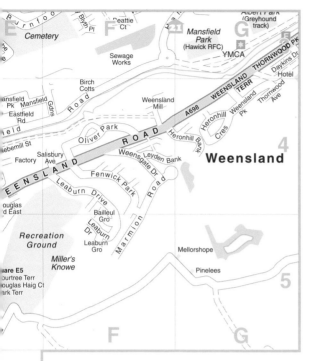

Mansfield Park	23 E4	Northcote Street (1)	22 D4	Renwick Terrace	22 C7	
Mansfield Road	22 E4	O'connell Street	22 D5	Rinkvale Cottages	22 E5	
Mansfield Square	22 E4	Old Manse Lane (3)	22 D6	Roadhead	22 C5	
Marmion Road	23 F5	Oliver Crescent	22 D5	Robson Court	21 F3	
Mart Street	22 E4	Oliver Park	23 F4	Rosalee Brae	22 C4	
Maxton Court	20 C3	Oliver Place	22 D5	Rosebank Road	22 C7	
Mayfield Drive	22 C4	Orchard Street	22 E6	Rosevale Cottages	22 E4	
Mayfield Park	22 D4	Orchard Terrace	22 E6	Rosevale Street	22 E4	
Melgund Place	22 D5	Orrock Place	22 D6	Roxburghe Drive	20 D3	
Melrose Court	20 E3	Overhall Crescent	22 A6	Ruberslaw Road	21 F2	
Mill Path	22 D6	Overhall Road	22 A6	St Cuthberts Court	22 D6	
Mill Port	22 D5	Oxnam Court	20 C3	St Cuthberts Terrace	22 D6	
Minto Place	22 E6	Park Grove	22 A6	St Georges Lane	22 C5	
Moat Crescent	22 C7	Park Street	22 E5	St Margarets Drive	22 C6	
Morrison Place	22 C6	Park Terrace (3)	22 E5	St Marys Place (1)	22 D6	
Myreslaw Court	22 C6	Park View	22 B6	St Ninians Road	22 E5	
Myreslaw Green (4)	22 C6	Princes Street	22 D4			
Noble Place	23 E4	Queen's Drive	21 G2			
North Bridge Street	22 D5	Raeson Park	20 D3			
		Ramsay Road	22 C7			

Salisbury Avenue	23 F4	Weensland Road	23 E4
Sandbed	22 D5	Weensland Terrace	23 G4
Scott Crescent	21 F2	Wellfield Bank	22 D4
Silver Street	22 D6	Wellfield Road	22 D4
Silverbuthall Road	20 D3	Wellington Court	22 C5
Slitrig Bank (2)	22 D6	Wellington Road	22 C5
Slitrig Crescent	22 D6	Wellogate Brae	22 E6
South Bright Street (4)	22 C6	Wellogate Place	22 D6
Station Buildings	22 D4	West End	22 C6
Stirches Road	20 C3	West Stewart Place	22 D4
Stonefield Place	22 D7	Wester Braid Road	22 D7
Sunnyhill Road	22 C5	Whins Cottage	21 E2
Tannage Close	22 D6	Whitehaugh Road	22 A5
Teviot Court	22 D6	Whitehaugh View	22 B7
Teviot Crescent	22 D5	Wilson Drive	21 F3
Teviot Road	22 D5	Wilton Crescent	22 D4
Teviotdale Court	21 F3	Wilton Glebe	21 E3
Teviotside Terrace (2)	22 D4	Wilton Hill	22 D4
Thornwood Avenue	23 G4	Wilton Hill Terrace	22 E4
Thornwood Park	21 G3	Wilton Lane	22 D4
Tower Dykeside (5)	22 D6	Wilton Park Road	22 A6
Tower Knowe (6)	22 D6	Wilton Park Road	22 B5
Trevelyn Terrace	22 C6	Wilton Path	22 D5
Trinity Street	22 E4	Yarrow Terrace	22 E5
Trystside	22 C7		
Twirlees Road	22 E5		
Twirlees Terrace	22 E5		
Under Damside	22 D5		
Union Street	22 E5		
Victoria Road	22 C5		
Village	22 D6		
Wallace Court	22 D4		
Walters Wynd	22 D5		
Waverley Terrace	22 E5		
Weensgate Drive	23 F4		
Weensland Park	23 G4		

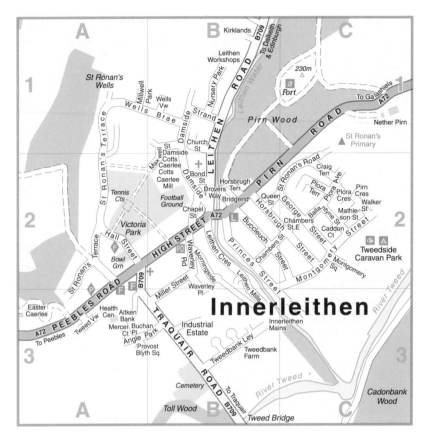

Index to Innerleithen

Aitken Bank	A3	Hall Street	A2	Pirn Road	B2
Angle Park	A3	High Street	B2	Plora Avenue	C2
Ballantyne Street	C2	Horsbrugh Street	B2	Plora Crescent	C2
Bond Street	B2	Horsbrugh Terrace	B2	Plora Terrace	C2
Buccleuch Street	B2	Leithen Crescent	B2	Princes Street	B2
Buchan Place	A3	Leithen Mills	B2	Provost Blyth Square	A3
Caddon Court	C2	Leithen Road	B2	Queen Street	B2
Caerlee Cottages	B2	Mathieson Street	C2	St Ronan's Road	C2
Chambers Street	B2	Maxwell Street	B2	St Ronan's Terrace	A2
Chambers Street East	C2	Mercer Court	A3	Strand	B1
Chapel Street	B2	Miller Street	B3	Traquair Road	B3
Church Street	B1	Millwell Park	A1	Tweed View	A3
Craig Terrace	C2	Montgomery Square	C2	Tweedbank Ley	B3
Damside	B1, B2	Montgomery Street	C2	Walker Street	C2
Damside Cottages	B2	Morningside	B2	Waverley Place	B2
Drovers Way	B2	Nursery Park	B1	Waverley Road	B2
George Street	C2	Peebles Road	A3	Wells Brae	A1
		Pirn Crescent	C2	Wells View	B1

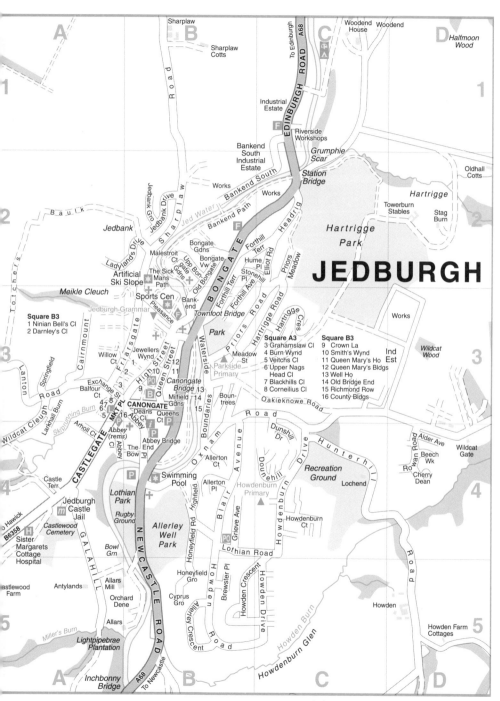

JEDBURGH

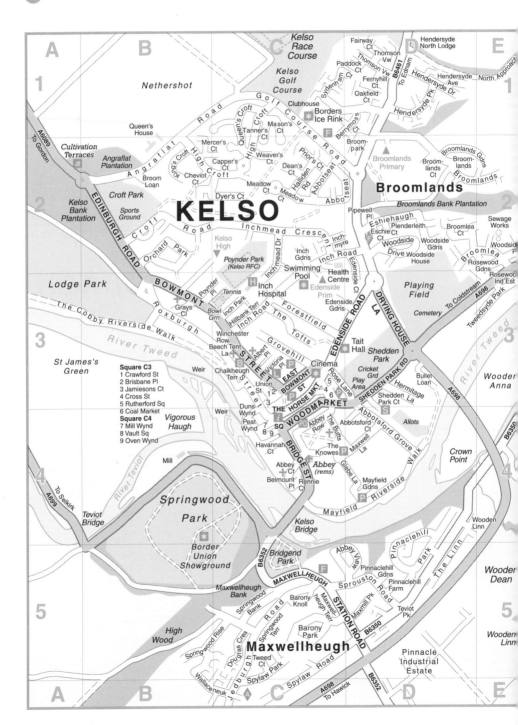

KELSO

Maxwellheugh

Broomlands

Kelso Race Course

Kelso Golf Course

Nethershot

Queen's House

Cultivation Terraces

Angraflat Plantation

Broom Loan

Cheviot Ct

Kelso Bank Plantation

Croft Park

Sports Ground

Orchard Park

Lodge Park

The Cobby Riverside Walk

River Tweed

St James's Green

Square C3
1 Crawford St
2 Brisbane Pl
3 Jamiesons Ct
4 Cross St
5 Rutherford Sq
6 Coal Market

Square C4
7 Mill Wynd
8 Vault Sq
9 Oven Wynd

Vigorous Haugh

Mill

Springwood Park

Border Union Showground

High Wood

Teviot Bridge

River Teviot

To Selkirk
A699

Maxwellheugh Bank

Springwood Bank

Springwood Rise

Douglas Cres

Edburgh

Wallaceneuk

Tweed Ct

Spylaw Park

B6352

Spylaw Road

A698 To Hawick

Golf Road

Queen's Croft

High Croft

King's Croft

Capper's Ct

Mercer's Ct

Weaver's Ct

Tanner's Ct

Mason's Ct

Clubhouse

Borders Ice Rink

Broom-park

Prior's Ct

Dean's Ct

Halliden Rd

Abbotseat

Meadow Ct

Dyer's Ct

Abbotseat

Pipewell Pl

Broomlands Primary

Broom-lands Ct

Broom-lands

Broomlands Gdns

Broomlands

Broomlands Bank Plantation

Eshiehaugh
Eschie Ct

Plenderleith

Broomlea Ct

Sewage Works

Woodside
Drive

Woodside Gdns

Woodside House

Broomlea

Woodsid
P

Rosewood Gdns

Rosewoo
Ind Est

Kelso High

Poynder Park (Kelso RFC)

Inchmead Cres

Inchmead Dr

Inch-myre

Inch Gdns

Inch Road

Edenside Ct

Edenside Prim

Edenside Gdns

Swimming Pool

Inch Hospital

Health Centre

Playing Field

Cemetery

To Coldstream
A698

Tweedsyde Park

River Tweed

Wooder Anna

Croft Road

Bowmont

Poynder Pl

Tennis

Inch Park

Bowl Grn

Hillbank Terr

Inch Road

Forestfield

The Totts

Grays Ct

Roxburgh

Winchester Row

Beech Tent La

Grovehill

Albert St

Victoria St

Street

Chalkheugh Terr

Union St

East Bowmont St

Cinema

Cricket Grd

Play Area

Rose Lane

Tait Hall

Shedden Park

Shedden Park Rd

Hermitage La

Shedden Park Ct

Bullet Loan

Abbotsford Grove

Allots

S

Crown Point

B6350

Weir

Weir

Duns Wynd

Peat Wynd

The Horse Mkt

Woodmarket

The Sq

Abbey Row

The Butts

Abbotsford

Maxwell La

Glebe La

Maxwell La

Havannah Ct

Bridge St

Abbey Ct

Belmount Pl

Abbey (rems)

Rennie Ct

Mayfield Gdns

Mayfield

P

Riverside Walk

A698

Kelso Bridge

Bridgend Park

Maxwellheugh

B6352

Abbey View

Sprouston Road

Pinnaclehill Gdns

Pinnaclehill Farm

Pinnaclehill

The Linn

Park

Wooden Linn

Wooder Dean

Barony Knoll

Barony Park

Maxwellheugh Terr

Station Road

B6350

Maxhill Pk

Teviot Pk

Wooden Linn

Pinnacle Industrial Estate

Fairway Ct

Thomson Vw

Paddock Ct

Thomson Vw

B6461

Sydenham Ct

Oakfield Ct

Fernyhill Ct

Hendersyde Pk

Hendersyde North Lodge

Hendersyde Ave

North Approach

To Ednam

Berrymoss Ct

Edinburgh Road

To Gordon
A6089

A6089

Bowmont

Drying House La

Edenside Road

Shedden Park Rd

The Knowes

P

ndex to Jedburgh

Abbey Bridge End	25 B4
Abbey Close	25 A4
Abbey Place	25 B3
Alder Avenue	25 D4
Allerley Crescent	25 B5
Allerton Court	25 B4
Allerton Place	25 B4
Atholl Court	25 A4
Balfour Court	25 A3
Bankend	25 B3
Bankend Path	25 B2
Bankend South	25 B2
Beech Walk	25 D4
Blackhills Close (7)	25 A3
Blair Avenue	25 B4
Bongate	25 B2
Bongate Gardens	25 B2
Bongate View	25 B2
Boundaries	25 B4
Bountrees	25 B3
Bow, The	25 B4
Brewster Place	25 B5
Burn Wynd (4)	25 A3
Cairnmount	25 A3
Canongate	25 B3
Castle Terrrace	25 A4
Castlegate	25 A4
Cherry Dean	25 D4
Cornelius Close (8)	25 A3
County Buildings (16)	25 B3
Crown Lane (9)	25 B3
Cypress Grove	25 B5
Darnley's Close (2)	25 B3
Deans Close	25 B3
Dounehill	25 C4
Dunshill Drive	25 C4
Edinburgh Road	25 C1
Elliot Road	25 C2
Exchange Street	25 A3
Forthill Avenue	25 B3
Forthill Terrace	25 B3
Friarsgate	25 B3
Galahill	25 A4
Grahamslaw Close (3)	25 A3
Grieve Avenue	25 B4
Hartrigge Crescent	25 C3
Hartrigge Road	25 C3
Headrig	25 C2
High Street	25 B3
Highfield	25 B4
Honeyfield Grove	25 B5
Honeyfield Road	25 B5
Howden Crescent	25 B5
Howden Drive	25 C5
Howden Road	25 B5
Howdenburn Court	25 C4
Howdenburn Drive	25 C4
Hume Place	25 B2
Hunthill Road	25 C4

Jedbank Drive	25 B2
Jedbank Grove	25 B2
Jewellers Wynd	25 B3
Larkhall Burn	25 A3
Ladylands Drive	25 A2
Lanton Road	25 A3
Lothian Road	25 B4
Malestroit Court	25 B2
Market Place	25 A3
Meadow Street	25 B3
Milfield Gardens	25 B3
Newcastle Road	25 B4
Ninian Bell's Close (1)	25 B3
Oakieknowe Road	25 C3
Old Bongate	25 B2
Old Bridge End (14)	25 B3
Oxnam Road	25 B4
Pleasance	25 B3
Priors Meadow	25 C2
Priors Road	25 B3
Queen Mary's Buildings (12)	25 B3
Queen Mary's House (11)	25 B3
Queen's Court	25 B3
Queens Street	25 B3
Richmond Row (15)	25 B3
Rowan Road	25 D4
Sharplaw Road	25 B2
Sick Man's Path	25 B2
Smith's Wynd (10)	25 B3
Springfield	25 A3
Stonehill Place	25 B2
Totchers Baulk	25 A3
Upper Bongate Gardens	25 B2
Upper Nag's Head Close (6)	25 A3
Veitch's Close (5)	25 A3
Waterside	25 B3
Well House (13)	25 B3
Wildcat Cleugh	25 A4
Willow Court	25 A3

Index to Kelso

Abbey Court	C4
Abbey Row	C4
Abbey View	C5
Abbotseat	C2
Abbotsford Court	D4
Abbotsford Grove	D4
Albert Place	C3
Angraflat Road	B2

Barony Knoll	C5
Barony Park	C5
Beech Tent Lane	C3
Belmount Place	C4
Berrymoss Court	D1
Bowmont Street	B3
Bridge Street	C4
Brisbane Place (2)	C3
Broom Loan	B2
Broomlands	D2
Broomlands Court	D2
Broomlands Gardens	D2
Broomlea	D2
Broomlea Court	D2
Broompark	D2
Bullet Loan	D3
Butts, The	C4
Capper's Court	C2
Chalkheugh Terrace	C3
Cheviot Court	B2
Coal Market (6)	C3
Cobby Riverside Walk, The	B3
Crawford Street (1)	C3
Croft Road	B2
Cross Street (4)	C3
Dean's Court	C2
Douglas Crescent	C5
Drying House Lane	D3
Duns Wynd	C4
Dyer's Court	C2
East Bowmont Street	C3
Edenside Court	D2
Edenside Gardens	C3
Edenside Road	C3
Edinburgh Road	B2
Eschie Court	D2
Eshiehaugh	D2
Fairway Court	D1
Fernyhill Court	D1
Forestfield	C3
Glebe Lane	D4
Golf Course Road	C1
Grays Close	B3
Grovehill	C3
Halliden Road	C2
Havannah Court	C4
Hendersyde Avenue	D1
Hendersyde Drive	D1
Hendersyde Park	D1
Hermitage Lane	D3
High Croft	B2, C2
Hillbank Terrace	C3
Horsemarket	C3
Inch Gardens	C2
Inch Park	C3
Inch Road	C2, C3
Inchmead Crescent	C2
Inchmead Drive	C2
Inchmyre	C2
Jamiesons Court (3)	C3

Jedburgh Road	B6
King's Croft	B2
Knowes, The	C4
Linn, The	D5
Mason's Court	C1
Maxmill Park	D5
Maxwell Lane	D4
Maxwellheugh	C5
Maxwellheugh Terrace	C5
Mayfield Riverside Walk	C4
Mayfield Gardens	D4
Meadow Court	C2
Mercer's Court	B2
Mill Wynd (7)	C4
North Approach	E1
Oakfield Court	D1
Orchard Park	B2
Oven Wynd (9)	C4
Paddock Court	D1
Peat Wynd	C4
Pinnaclehill Farm	D5
Pinnaclehill Gardens	D5
Pinnaclehill Park	D5
Pipewell Place	D2
Plenderleith Court	D2
Poynder Place	B3
Prior's Court	C2
Queen's Croft	C2
Rennie Court	C4
Rose Lane	C3
Rosewood Gardens	E2
Roxburgh Street	B3
Rutherford Square (5)	C3
Shedden Park Court	D3
Shedden Park Road	D3
Springwood Bank	C5
Springwood Rise	B5
Springwood Terrace	C5
Sprouston Road	C5
Spylaw Park	C6
Spylaw Road	C6
Square, The	C4
Station Road	C5
Sydenham Court	C1
Tanner's Court	C1
Teviot Park	D5
Thomson View	D1
Tofts, The	C3
Tweed Court	C5
Tweedsyde Park	E3
Union Street	C3
Vault Square (8)	C4
Victoria Place	C3
Wallaceneuk	C5
Weaver's Court	C2
Winchester Row	C3
Wooden Linn	D4
Woodmarket	C4
Woodside Drive	D2
Woodside Gardens	D2
Woodside Park	E2

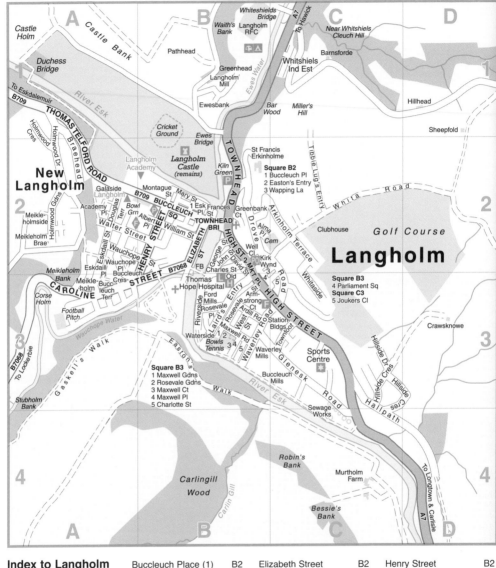

Index to Langholm

Academy Place	A2		
Albert Place	B2		
Alma Place	B2		
Ardill Road	B3		
Arkinholm Terrace	C2		
Armstrong Court	B3		
Braehead Crescent	A1		
Buccleuch Crescent	A3		
Buccleuch Mills	C3		

Buccleuch Place (1)	B2	
Buccleuch Square	B2	
Buccleuch Terrace	A3	
Caroline Street	A3	
Charles Street Old	B2	
Charlotte Street (5)	B3	
David Street	B2	
Douglas Terrace	A2	
Drove Road	B2	
Easton's Walk	B3	
Easton's Entry (2)	B2	

Elizabeth Street	B2
Esk Place	B2
Eskdaill Place	A2
Eskdaill Street	A2
Ford Mills	B3
Frances Street	B2
Galaside	A2
George Street	B2
Glenesk Road	C3
Greenbank Court	B2
Hallpath	C3

Henry Street	B2
High Street	B2, B3
Hillside Crescent	C3
Hillside Drive	C3
Holmwood Drive	A2
Holmwood Gardens	A2
Holmwood	A1
John Street	B2
Joukers Close (5)	C3
Kirk Wynd	B2
Laird's Entry	B3

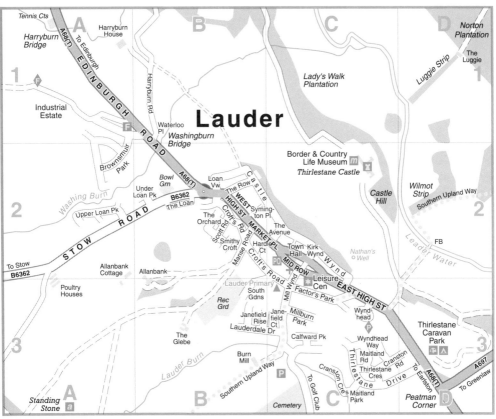

Lauder

Market Place	B2	Walter Street	A2	Croft's Road	B2	Stow Road	A2
Mary Street	B2	Wapping Lane (3)	B2	East High Street	C3	Symington Place	B2
Maxwell Court (3)	B3	Waterside	B3	Edinburgh Road	A1	Thirlestane Crescent	C3
Maxwell Gardens (1)	B3	Wauchope Place	A2	Factor's Park	C3	Thirlestane Drive	C3
Maxwell Place (4)	B3	Wauchope Street	A2	Harryburn Road	B1	Under Loan Park	B2
Maxwell Road	B3	Waverley Mills	B3	Janefield Court	C3	Upper Loan Park	A2
Meikleholm Brae	A2	Waverley Road	B3	Janefield Rise	B3	Waterloo Place	B1
Meikleholm	A3	Well Close	B2	Kirk Wynd	C2	West High Street	B2
Meikleholmside	A2	West Street	B3	Lauderdale Drive	B3	Wyndhead	C3
Montague Street	B2	Whita Road	C2	Loan, The	B2	Wyndhead Way	C3
Parliament	B3	Whitaside	C3	Loan View	B2		
Square (4)		William Street	B2	Maitland Park	C3		
Riverside	B3			Maitland Road	C3		
Rosevale Gardens (2)	B3			Manse Road	B2		
Rosevale Place	B3			Market Place	B2		
Rosevale Street	B3			Mid Row	C2		
Station Buildings	C3	**Index to Lauder**		Mill Wynd	C3		
Thomas Telford	A1			Millburn Park	C3		
Road		Avenue, The	C2	Orchard, The	B2		
Tibbie Lug's Entry	C2	Brownsmuir Park	A2	Row, The	B2		
Townfoot	C3	Castle Wynd	B2	Scott Road	B2		
Townhead Bridge	B2	Cranston Crescent	C3	Smithy Croft	B2		
Townhead	B2	Cranston Road	C3	South Gardens	B3		

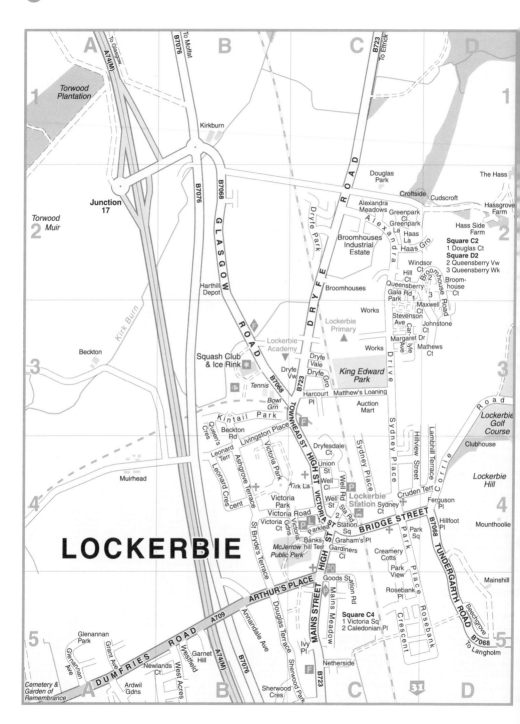

LOCKERBIE

Square C2
1 Douglas Ct

Square D2
2 Queensberry Vw
3 Queensberry Wk

Square C4
1 Victoria Sq
2 Caledonian Pl

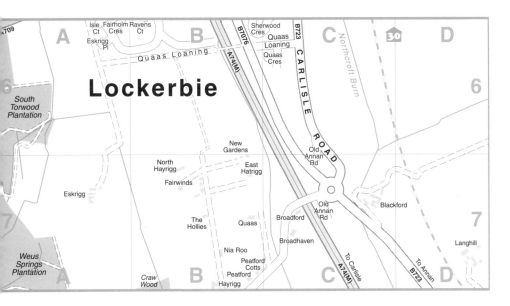

Index to Lockerbie

lexandra Drive	C2	Gala Park	C2	Matthew's Loaning	C3	Townhead Street	C3
lexandra Meadows	C2	Gardiners Close	C4	Maxwell Court	C3	Tundergarth Road	D4
nnandale Avenue	B5	Glasgow Road	B2	Netherside	C5	Union Street	C4
rdwil Gardens	A5	Glenannan Avenue	A5	Newlands Court	B5	Vallance Drive	A5
rthur's Place	B5	Glenannan Park	A5	Old Annan Road	C7	Victoria Court	B4
shgrove Terrace	B4	Goods Station Road	C5	Park Place	C4	Victoria Gardens	C4
ankshill Terrace	C4	Graham's Place	C4	Park Square	C4	Victoria Park	B4
eckton Road	B3	Grant Avenue	A5	Park View	C4	Victoria Road	B4
eechgrove	D5	Greenpark Close	C2	Parklea	C4	Victoria Square (1)	C4
ridge Street	C4	Greenpark Lane	C2	Quaas Loaning	B6	Victoria Street	C4
roomhouse Court	D2	Haas Grove	C2	Quaas Crescent	C6	Well Close	C4
roomhouse Road	D2	Haas Lane	C2	Queen's Crescent	B3	Well Road	C4
aledonian Place (2)	C4	Harcourt Place	C3	Queensberry Road	C2	Well Street	C4
arlisle Road	C6	High Street	C4	Queensberry	D2	West Acres	B5
arlyle Avenue	C3	Hill Court	C2	View (2)		Wesfield	B5
orrie Road	D4	Hillfoot Place	D3	Queensberry	D2	Windsor Court	C2
reamery Cottages	C4	Hillview Street	C4	Walk (3)			
ruden Terrace	C4	Isle Court	A6	Ravens Court	B5		
ouglas Court (1)	C2	Ivy Place	C5	Rosebank Crescent	D5		
ouglas Terrace	B5	Johnstone Court	D3	Rosebank Place	C5		
ryfe Grove	C3	Kintail Park	B3	St Bryde's Terrace	B4		
ryfe Park	C2	Kirk Lane	C4	Sherwood	B5, B6		
ryfe Road	C3	Lambhill Terrace	D3	Crescent			
ryfe Vale	C3	Leonard Crescent	B4	Sherwood Park	C5		
ryfe View	C3	Leonard Terrace	B4	Station Road	C4		
ryfesdale Court	C4	Livingston Place	B4	Station Square	C4		
umfries Road	A5	Mains Meadow	C5	Stevenson Avenue	C3		
skrigg Place	A6	Mains Street	C5	Sydney Place	C4		
airholm Crescent	A6	Margaret Drive	C3	Sydney Court	C4		
erguson Place	D4	Mathews Court	D3	Sydney Place	C3		

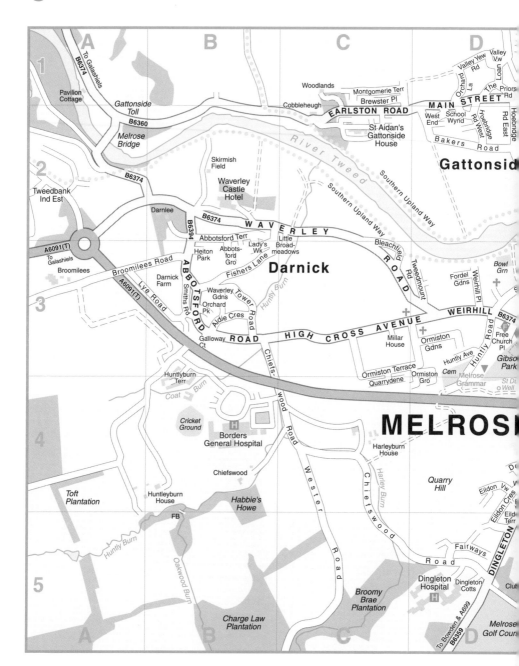

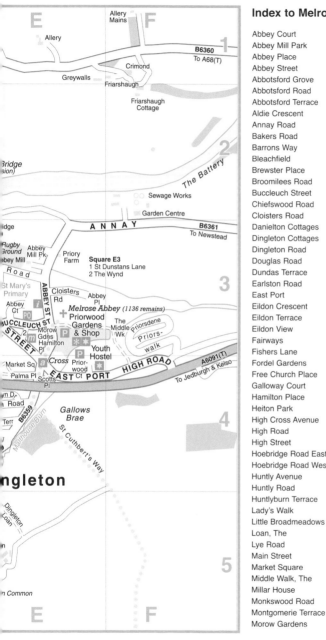

Index to Melrose

Abbey Court	E3		Newlyn Drive	E4
Abbey Mill Park	E3		Newlyn Road	E4
Abbey Place	E3		Orchard Lane	D1
Abbey Street	E3		Orchard Park	B3
Abbotsford Grove	B3		Ormiston Gardens	D3
Abbotsford Road	B3		Ormiston Grove	D3
Abbotsford Terrace	B2		Ormiston Terrace	C3
Aldie Crescent	B3		Palma Place	E4
Annay Road	E3		Priors Road	D1
Bakers Road	D2		Priorsdene	F3
Barrons Way	D4		Priorswalk	F3
Bleachfield	C3		Priorwood Court	E4
Brewster Place	C1		Quarrydene	C4
Broomilees Road	A3		St Dunstans Lane (1)	E3
Buccleuch Street	E3		St Dunstans Park	E3
Chiefswood Road	B3, C4		St Mary's Road	D3
Cloisters Road	E3		School Wynd	D2
Danielton Cottages	D5		Scotts Place	E4
Dingleton Cottages	D5		Smiths Road	B3
Dingleton Road	D5		Tower Road	B3
Douglas Road	D4		Tweedmount Road	D3
Dundas Terrace	E4		Valley View	D1
Earlston Road	C2		Valley Yew Road	D1
East Port	E4		Waverley Gardens	B3
Eildon Crescent	D5		Waverley Road	B2
Eildon Terrace	D5		Weirhill	D3
Eildon View	D4		Weirhill Place	D3
Fairways	D5		Wembley Terrace	D4
Fishers Lane	B3		West End	D2
Fordel Gardens	D3		Wester Road	C4
Free Church Place	D3		Wynd, The (2)	E3
Galloway Court	B3			
Hamilton Place	E3			
Heiton Park	B3			
High Cross Avenue	C3			
High Road	F4			
High Street	D3			
Hoebridge Road East	D2			
Hoebridge Road West	D2			
Huntly Avenue	D3			
Huntly Road	D4			
Huntlyburn Terrace	B3			
Lady's Walk	B3			
Little Broadmeadows	C2			
Loan, The	D1			
Lye Road	A3			
Main Street	D1			
Market Square	E4			
Middle Walk, The	F3			
Millar House	C3			
Monkswood Road	D1			
Montgomerie Terrace	C1			
Morow Gardens	E3			

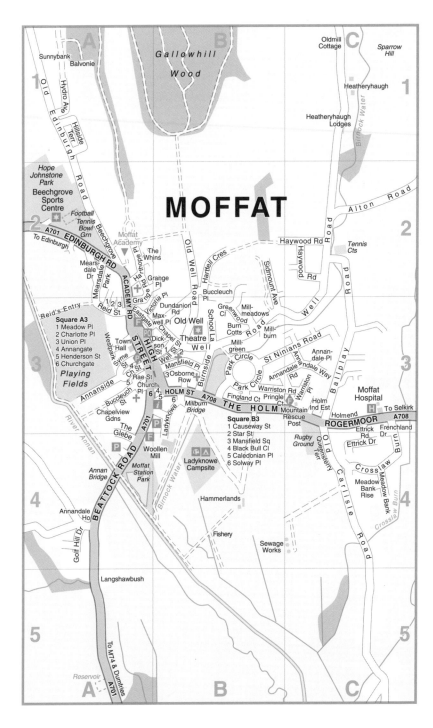

Sunnybank
Balvonie
Gallowhill Wood
Oldmill Cottage
Sparrow Hill
Heatheryhaugh
Heatheryhaugh Lodges
Birnock Water

Old Edinburgh Road
Hydro Ave
Hillside Terr

Hope Johnstone Park
Beechgrove Sports Centre
Football
Tennis
Bowl
Grn
A701 To Edinburgh
EDINBURGH RD
Beechgrove
Moffat Academy
The Whins

MOFFAT

Alton Road
Haywood Rd
Haywood Rd
Tennis Cts
Well Road
Road

Mears-dale Dr
Mearsdale
Park
ACADEMY RD
Harthpe Pl
Penang
Grange Pl
Hartfell Cres
Sidmount Ave

Reid's Entry
Reid St
Gra
Victoria Pl
Chapel St
Buccleuch Pl
Dundanion Rd
Old Well Road
Greenwood Cl
Mill-meadows

Square A3
1 Meadow Pl
2 Charlotte Pl
3 Union Pl
4 Annangate
5 Henderson St
6 Churchgate

Max-well Pl
Dick-son St
Old Well
Theatre
Well
School La
Burn Cotts
Mill-burn
Mill-green
Mill-meadows

Playing Fields
Annanside
Town Hall
Westpark St
Syme St
HIGH STREET
Eastgate
Mansfield Pl
Well St
Park Circle
St Ninians Road
Annan-dale Pl
Ballplay Road

Ch St
Rae St
Church Pl
3 Osborne Row
Burnside
Park Circle
Annandale Way
Annandale Rd
Warriston

Buccleuch St
Chapelview Gdns
The Glebe
HOLM ST
A708
Millburn Bridge
THE HOLM
Finland Ct
Warriston Rd
Pringle Ct
Holm Ind Est
Moffat Hospital
H To Selkirk

River Annan
BEATTOCK ROAD
A701
Ladyknowe
Woollen Mill
Square B3
1 Causeway St
2 Star St
3 Mansfield Sq
4 Black Bull Cl
5 Caledonian Pl
6 Solway Pl
Mountain Rescue Post
Holmend
ROGERMOOR
A708
Ettrick Rd
Frenchland Dr
Ettrick Dr

Annan Bridge
Moffat Station Park
Birnock Water
Ladyknowe Campsite
Rugby Ground
Queensberry Terr
Old Carlisle Road
Crosslaw Burn
Meadow Bank Rise
Meadow Bank
Crosslaw Burn

Annandale Ho
Golf Hill Dr
Hammerlands
Fishery
Sewage Works

Langshawbush

Reservoir
To M74 & Dumfries
A701

Index to Moffat

Academy Road	A2
Alton Road	C2
Annandale Place	C3
Annandale Road	C3
Annandale Way	C3
Annangate (4)	A3
Annanside	A3
Ballplay Road	C3
Beattock Road	A4
Beechgrove	A2
Black Bull Close (4)	B3
Buccleuch Place	B2
Buccleuch Street	A3
Burn Cottages	B3
Burnside	B3
Caledonian Place (5)	B3
Causeway Street (1)	B3
Chapel Street	B3
Chapleview Gardens	A3
Charlotte Place (2)	A3
Church Place	A3
Church Street	A3
Churchgate (6)	A3
Crosslaw Burn	C4
Dickson Street	B3
Dundanion Road	B3
Eastgate	A3
Edinburgh Road	A2
Ettrick Drive	C4
Ettrick Road	C3
Fingland Court	B3
Frenchland Drive	C3
Glebe, The	A4
Golf Hill Drive	A4
Grange Place	B2
Grange Road	A3
Greenwood Close	B3
Hartfell Crescent	B2
Harthope Place	A2
Haywood Road	C2
Henderson	A3
Street (5)	
High Street	A3
Hillside Terrace	A1
Holm Street	B3
Holm, The	B3
Holmend	C3
Hydro Avenue	A1
Ladyknowe	B3
Mansfield Place	B3
Mansfield Square (3)	B3
Maxwell Place	B3
Meadow Bank Rise	C4
Meadow Bank	C4
Meadow Place (1)	A3
Mearsdale Drive	A2
Mearsdale Park	A2
Mill Road	C3
Millburn	B3
Millgreen	B3
Millmeadows	B3
Old Carlisle Road	C4

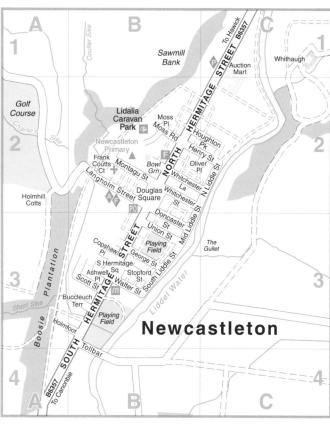

Newcastleton

Old Edinburgh Road	A1
Old Well Road	B2
Osborne Row	B3
Park Circle	B3
Pringle Court	B3
Queensferry Terrace	C4
Rae Street	A3
Reid Street	A3
Reid's Entry	A3
Rogermoor	C3
St Ninians Road	B3
School Lane	B3
Sidmount Avenue	B2
Solway Place (6)	B3
Star Street (2)	B3
Syme Street	A3
Union Place (3)	A3
Victoria Place	A3
Warriston Place	C3
Warriston Road	B3
Well Road	B3
Well Street	B3
Westpark	A3
Whins, The	A2

Index to Newcastleton

Ashwell Place	B3
Buccleuch Terrace	B3
Copshaw Place	B3
Doncaster Street	B3
Douglas Square	B2
Frank Coutts Court	B2
George Street	B3
Henry Street	B2
Holmfoot	A3
Holmhill Cottages	A2
Houghton Park	C2
Langholm Street	B2
Mid Liddle Street	B3
Montagu Street	B2
Moss Place	B2
Moss Road	B2
North Hermitage	B2
Street	
North Liddle Street	C2
Oliver Place	C2
Scott Street	B3
South Hermitage	B3
Square	
South Hermitage	B3
Street	
South Liddle Street	B3
Stopford Street	B3
Tollbar	B4
Union Street	B3
Walter Street	B3
Whitchester Lane	B2
Whitchester Street	B2

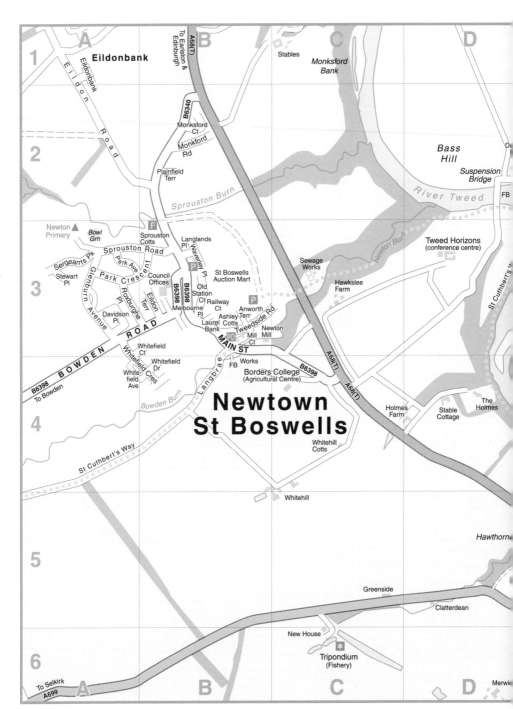

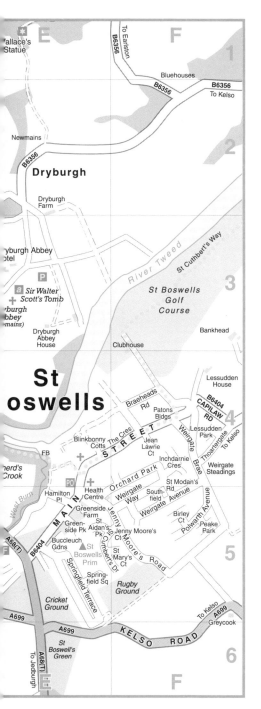

Index to Newtown St Boswells & St Boswells

Anworth Terrace	B3	Stewart Place	A3
Ashley Cottages	B3	Thoartergate	F4
Birley Court	F5	Tweedside Road	B3
Blinkbonny Cottages	E4	Waverley Place	B3
Bowden Road	A4	Weirgate Avenue	F5
Brae Heads Road	F4	Weirgate Brae	F4
Buccleuch Chase	D5	Weirgate Way	F5
Buccleuch Gardens	E5	Whitefield Avenue	A4
Capilaw Road	F4	Whitefield Court	B3
Crescent, The	F4	Whitefield Crescent	A3
Davidson Place	A3	Whitefield Drive	B4
Eildon Road	A1		
Eildon Terrace	B3		
Eildonbank	A1		
Glenburn Avenue	A3		
Greenside Park	E5		
Hamilton Place	E5		
Inchdarnie Crescent	F4		
Jean Lawrie Court	F4		
Jenny Moore's Court	F5		
Jenny Moore's Road	F5		
Kelso Road	F6		
Langbrae	B4		
Langlands Place	B3		
Laurel Bank	B3		
Lessudden Park	F4		
Main Street	B3		
(Newton St Boswells)			
Main Street	E5		
(St Boswells)			
Melbourne Place	B3		
Mill Court	B3		
Monkford Road	B2		
Monksford Court	B2		
Old Station Court	B3		
Orchard Park	F4		
Park Avenue	A3		
Park Crescent	A3		
Patons Buildings	F4		
Peake Park	F5		
Plainfield Terrace	B2		
Polwarth Avenue	F5		
Railway Court	B3		
Roxburghe Place	A3		
St Aidan's Park	E5		
St Cuthbert's Drive	E5		
St Mary's Court	F5		
St Modan's Road	F5		
Sergeants Park	A3		
Southfield	F5		
Springfield Square	E5		
Springfield Terrace	E5		
Sprouston Cottages	B3		
Sprouston Road	A3		

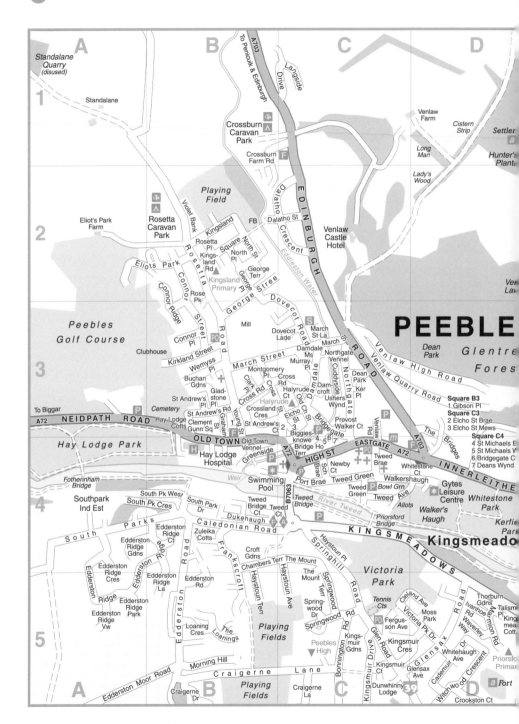

PEEBLES

Square B3
1 Gibson Pl

Square C3
2 Elcho St Brae
3 Elcho St Mews

Square C4
4 St Michaels B
5 St Michaels W
6 Bridgegate C
7 Deans Wynd

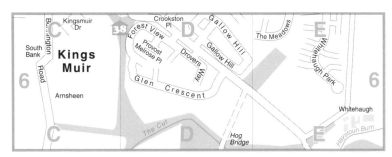

Index to Peebles

Biggiesknowe	C4	Edinburgh Road	C2	Newby Court	C4
Bonnington Road	C6	Elcho Street	C3	North Place	B2
Bridge House Terrace	C4	Elcho Street Brae	C3	North Street	B2
Bridgegate	C3	Eliots Park	B2	Northgate	C3
Bridgegate Court (6)	C4	Fergusson Avenue	C5	Northgate Vennel	C3
Bridges, The	D3	Forest View	D6	Old Church Road	C3
Buchan Gardens	B3	Frankscroft	B4	Old Town	B4
Cademuir Drive	D5	Gallow Hill	D6	Old Town Vennel	B4
Caledonian Road	B4	George Place	B2	Port Brae	C4
Chambers Terrace	B4	George Street	B3	Provost Melrose Place	D6
Clark Place	B3	George Terrace	B2	Provost Walker Court	C3
Cleland Avenue	C5	Gibson Place (1)	B3	Rose Park	B2
Clement Gunn Square	B3	Gladstone Place	B3	Rosetta Place	B2
Connor Place	B3	Glen Crescent	D6	Rosetta Road	B2
Connor Ridge	B2	Glen Road	C5	Rowan Court	E5
Connor Street	B2	Glensax Avenue	D5	St Andrew's Court	B3
Craigerne Crescent	B6	Glensax Road	D5	St Andrew's Place	B3
Craigerne Drive	B5	Graham Street	B3	St Andrew's Road	B3
Craigerne Lane	B5, C5	Greenside	B4	St Michaels Bank (4)	C4
Croft Gardens	B4	Halyrude Court	C3	St Michaels Wynd (5)	C4
Crookston Court	D5	Hay Lodge Cottages	B3	School Brae	C4
Crookston Place	D6	Haystoun Avenue	C5	South Park Crescent	A4
Cross Road	B3	Haystoun Place	C4	South Park Drive	B4
Cross Street	B3	Haystoun Terrace	B5	South Park West	B4
Crossburn Farm Road	B1	High Street	C4	South Parks	A4
Crossland Crescent	B3	Innerleithen Road	D4	Springhill Road	C4
Cuddyside	C3	Ivanhoe Road	D5	Springwood Drive	C5
Dalatho Crescent	C2	Ker Place	C3	Springwood Terrace	C5
Dalatho Street	C2	Kingsland Road	B2	Springwood Road	C5
Damcroft	C3	Kingsland Square	B2	Standalane	A1
Damdale	C3	Kingsmeadows Cottages	D5	Talisman Place	D5
Damdale Mews	C3	Kingsmeadows Gardens	D5	Thornburn Gardens	D5
Dean Park	C3	Kingsmeadows Road	C4	Tweed Avenue	C4
Deans Wynd (7)	C4	Kingsmuir Court	C5	Tweed Brae	C4
Dovecot Lade	C3	Kingsmuir Crescent	C5	Tweed Bridge Court	B4
Dovecot Road	C3	Kingsmuir Drive	C5	Tweed Court	C4
Drovers Way	D6	Kingsmuir Gardens	C5	Tweed Green	C4
Dukehaugh	B4	Kingsway	D5	Ushers Wynd	C3
Eastgate	C4	Kirkland Street	B3	Venlaw High Road	C3
Edderston Moor Road	A5	Langside Drive	C1	Venlaw Quarry Road	C3
Edderston Ridge	A5	Loaning Crescent	B5	Venlaw Road	C3
Edderston Ridge Court	B4	Loanings, The	B5	Victoria Park Drive	C5
Edderston Ridge Crescent	A4	March Street	B3, C3	Violet Bank	B2
		March Street Lane	C3	Walker's Haugh	C4
Edderston Ridge Gardens	A4	Marmion Road	D5	Waverley Way	D5
		Meadows, The	E5	Wemyss Place	B3
Edderston Ridge Lane	B5	Montgomery Place	B3	Whitehaugh Avenue	D5
Edderston Ridge Park	A5	Morning Hill	B5	Whitehaugh Park	E5, E6
Edderston Ridge View	A5	Moss Park	D5	Whitestone Court	D4
Edderston Road	B5	Mount, The	C4	Witchwood Crescent	D5
		Murray Place	C3	Young Street	B3
		Neidpath Road	A3	Zuleika Cottages	B4

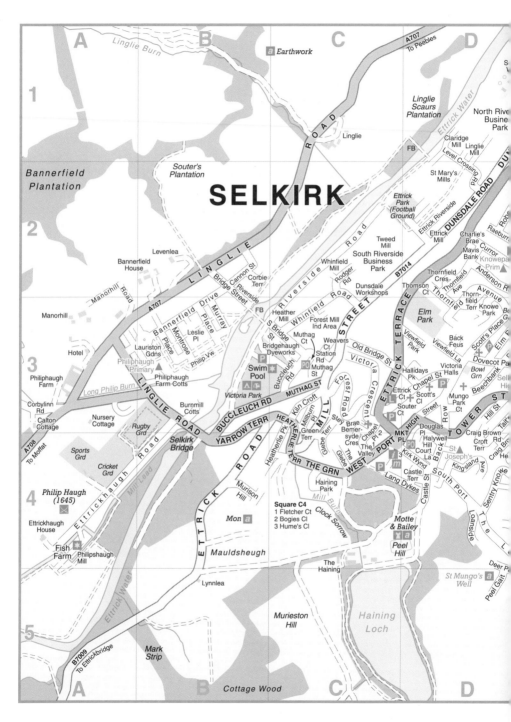

SELKIRK

Bannerfield Plantation

Souter's Plantation

Linglie Burn

Earthwork

A707 To Peebles

Linglie

Linglie Scaurs Plantation

North River Busine Park

Claridge Mill
Linglie Mill
Level Crossing
St Mary's Mills
FB
Ettrick Riverside
Charlie's Brae
Curror
Mavis Bank
Knowepa
Prim

Ettrick Park (Football Ground)
Ettrick Mill

Levenlea

Bannerfield House

Manorhill Road

Manorhill

Hotel

Philiphaugh Farm

Corbylinn Rd

Calton Cottage

A708 To Moffat

Sports Grd

Cricket Grd

Philip Haugh (1645)

Ettrickhaugh House

Fish Farm

Philipshaugh Mill

Cannon St
Corbie Terr
Bridge Street
Murray Place
Montrose Place
Leslie Pl
Lauriston Gdns
Philip Vw
Philiphaugh Primary
Philiphaugh Farm Cotts
Long Philip Burn

Bannerfield Drive

LINGLIE

Riverside

Road

Whinfield Mill
Rodger Rd
Dunsdale Workshops
Heather Mill
Forest Mill Ind Area
Muthag Ct
Bridgehaugh Dyeworks
Weavers Ct
Station Rd
Muthag St

Tweed Mill
South Riverside Business Park

B7014

Thomson Ct

Thornfield Cres.
Thornfield Ave
Thorn-field Terr
Elm Park

Anderson R
Avenue
Knowe Park
Back Feus
Scott's Place
Elm L
Dovecot Pa
Bowl Grn
Beechbank
Selk

Viewfield Park
Viewfield La
Victoria Halls
Victoria Park
Chapel St
Scott's Cl
Souter
Ettrick Ct
Mungo Park Ct

FB

Swim Pool
Victoria Park

Burnmill Cotts

BUCCLEUGH RD

YARROW TERR

Selkirk Bridge

Rugby Grd

Nursery Cottage

Ettrickhaugh

Mill Lead

MUTHAG ST

HEATHERLIE TERR

Kiln Croft
Millburn
Green Terr

THE GRN

Haining Park

Murison Hill

Mauldsheugh

Lynnlea

Mark Strip

Mon

Clock Sorrow

Square C4
1 Fletcher Ct
2 Bogies Cl
3 Hume's Cl

The Haining

Murieston Hill

Victoria Crescent
Old Bridge St
Hallidays Pk
Chapel St
Brae
Bemersyde Cres
The Glebe
Chapel Pl
The Valley

Halywell Hill
Douglas Pl
Kirk Wynd
Castle Terr
Lang Dykes

Haining Loch

Craig Brown
Croft Terr
St Joseph's
Kingsland

Motte & Bailey
Peel Hill

The Haining

St Mungo's Well

Deer Pk
Peel Gait

Cottage Wood

B7009 To Ettrickbridge

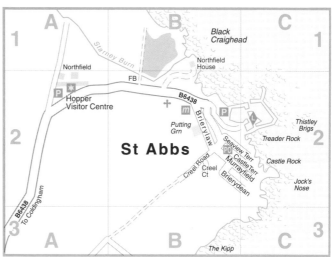

St Abbs

Index to Selkirk

Anderson Road	D2	
Ashybank	E1	
Back Feus	D3	
Back Row	D4	
Balnagowan Road	D2	
Bannerfield Drive	B3	
Beechbank	D3	
Bemersyde Crescent	C3	
Bleachfield Road	D2	
Bogies Close (2)	C4	
Bridge Street	B2	
Bridgelands Road	E1	
Buccleuch Road	B3	
Cannon Street	B2	
Castle Street	D4	
Castle Terrace	D4	
Chapel Place	C3	
Chapel Street	D3	
Charlie's Brae	D2	
Clifton Road	D3	
Corbie Terrace	B2	
Corbylinn Road	A3	
Court Lane	D4	
Craig Brown Avenue	D4	
Craig Brown Road	D4	
Croft Terrace	D4	
Curror Street	D2	
Deer Park	D4	
Douglas Place	D4	
Dovecot Lane	D3	
Dovecot Park	D3	
Dunsdale Haugh	D2	
Dunsdale Road	D2	
Eastfield Road	E2	
Elm Row	D3	

Ettrick Court	C3
Ettrick Riverside	D2
Ettrick Road	B4
Ettrick Terrace	C3
Ettrickhaugh Road	A4
Fairfield Crescent	E2
Fairfield Drive	E2
Fletcher Court (1)	C4
Forrest Road	C3
Gaitschaw Lane	E2
Glebe Terrace	C4
Glebe, The	C4
Green, The	C4
Goslaw Green	E3
Goslawdales	E3
Green Terrace	C3
Haining Park	C4
Hallidays Park	D3
Halywell Hill	D4
Heatherlie Park	C4
Heatherlie Terrace	C3
Heathpark Place	D4
High School Lane	E3
High Street	D3
Hill Street	D3
Hillside Terrace	E4
Hillview Crescent	E4
Hume's Close (3)	D4
Kiln Croft	C3
Kingsland Avenue	D4
Kirk Wynd	D4
Knowe Park	D3
Ladylands Drive	D4
Ladylands Terrace	D4
Ladyschaw Drive	E2
Ladywood	E4
Lang Dykes	C4

Lauriston Gardens	A3
Leslie Place	B3
Level Crossing Road	D1
Linglie Road	A3
Linglie Road	B2
Loan, The	D4
Loanside	D4
Manorhill Road	A3
Market Place	C4
Mavis Bank	D2
Mill Street	C2
Millburn Place	C3
Montrose Place	B3
Mungo Park Court	D3
Murison Hill	B2
Murray Place	B3
Muthag Court	C3
Muthag Street	C3
Old Bridge Road	C3
Peel Gait	E5
Philip View	B3
Philiphaugh Farm Cottages	B3
Raeburn Lane	E2
Raeburn Meadow	D2
Raeburn Place	E2
Riverside	B2
Riverside Road	C2
Roberts Avenue	D2
Rogers Road	C2
Rosebank Drive	E3
Russell Place	E4
Scott Crescent	E3
Scott's Close	D3
Scott's Place	D3
Sentry Knowe	D2
Shawburn Road	D2
Shawpark Crescent	E3

Shawpark Drive	E2
Shawpark Road	E2
Souter Court	C3
South Bridge Street	C3
South Port	D4
Spion Kop	E1
Station Road	C3
Stey Brae	C3
Taits Hill	D3
Thirlestane Terrace	E2
Thomson Court	D3
Thornfield Avenue	D2
Thornfield Crescent	D2
Thornfield Terrace	D3
Tower Street	D3
Valley, The	C4
Victoria Crescent	C3
Victoria Halls	D3
Viewfield Lane	D3
Viewfield Park	D3
Weavers Court	C3
West Port	C4
Whinfield Road	C3
Yarrow Terrace	B4

Index to St Abbs

Brierydean	B2
Brierylaw	B2
Castle Terrace	B2
Creel Court	B2
Creel Road	B2
Murrayfield	B2
Seaview Terrace	B2

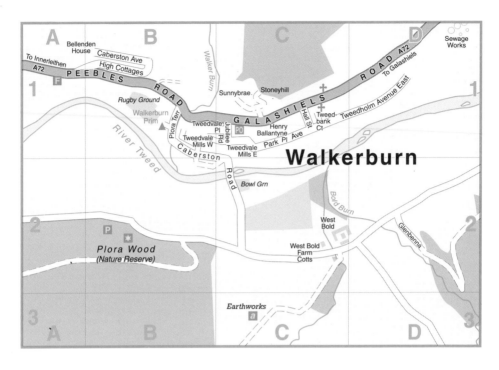

Index to Walkerburn

Caberston Avenue	B1	
Caberston Road	B1	
Galashiels Road	C1	
Glenbenna	D2	
Hall Street	C1	
Henry Ballantyne Place	C1	
High Cottages	B1	
Jubilee Road	C1	
Park Avenue	C1	
Peebles Road	A1	
Plora Terrace	B1	
Tweedbank Court	C1	
Tweedholm Avenue East	C1	
Tweedvale Mills East	C1	
Tweedvale Mills West	B1	
Tweedvale Place	B1	

Index to Berwick-upon-Tweed

Adams Drive	7 F9	
Albert Place	5 F5	
Albert Road	7 H9	
Alderbush Close	6 D9	
Anderson Court (5)	7 F6	
Askew Crescent	7 F8	
Ava Lodge	5 E4	
Avenue, The	7 G6	
Bank Hill	5 F5	
Bay Terrace	7 G6	
Bede Avenue	5 E3	
Bell Tower Park	5 F5	
Billendean Road	7 F8	
Billendean Terrace	7 F8	
Blackhall Court	7 E10	
Blakewell Gardens	7 E6	
Blakewell Lane	7 E6	
Blakewell Street	7 E6	
Blenheim Place	7 H9	
Bowers Crescent	7 E6	
Braeside	7 E9	
Breakneck Steps	5 E5	
Brewery Bank	7 E7	
Brewery Lane	7 E7	
Brickfield Lodge	7 E9	
Bridge Court	7 E6	
Bridge End	7 F6	
Bridge Street	7 F6	
Bridge Terrace	7 F6	
Brucegate	5 F5	
Callers Court	6 D9	
Carrick Close	5 E3	
Castle Drive	5 E4	
Castle Terrace	4 D4	
Castlegate	5 F5	
Cemetery Lane	7 E9	
Chapel Street	5 F5	
Chiltern Close	6 D9	
Church Road	7 E7	
Church Street	7 F6	
Cleet Court	7 G6	
Clove Court	6 D9	
Coastguard Cottages	7 G6	
College Place	5 F5	
Commercial Road	7 G8	
Cornhill Road	6 C8	
Cornwall Avenue	6 C9	
Countess of Buchan Way	5 E3	
Cow Road	7 H9	
Coxons Lane	5 F5	
Crawford's Alley	5 F5	
Crescent, The	7 H9	
Crispin Road	5 E3	
Croft, The	6 C9	
Crosthwaite Terrace	7 F8	
Dean Drive	7 E8	
Dean Drive	7 E9	
Devon Terrace	7 G6	
Dewars Lane	7 F6	
Dock Road	7 F7	
Douglas Close	5 E3	
Drivers Lane (4)	7 F6	
Duns Road	4 B3	
East Ord Farm Cottages	6 B8	
East Street	7 G8	
Eastcliffe	7 G9	
Easter Wynd (3)	7 F6	
Eastern Lane	7 F6	
Eildon View	7 E10	
Etal Road	6 D10	
Etal Road	7 E8	
Etal Way	7 E9	
Falloden Terrace	7 F8	
Farne Road	7 F8	
Fetter's Lane	7 F7	
Ford Court (7)	7 F6	
Foul Ford (8)	7 F6	
Freeman's Court	5 F5	
Gallow Knowe	5 E4	
Glamis Hill	5 E3	
Glenside Park	6 B9	
Golden Square	7 F6	
Goldstone	6 D9	
Grand Loaning	4 A1	
Grangeburn Close	6 D9	
Green, The	6 B8	
Greenside Avenue	5 F5	
Greenway	6 C9	
Greenwood	6 D8	

Index to Galashiels

Grove Gardens South	7 E9	Mount Road	7 F7	Sandstell Road
Grove Gardens	7 E8	Ner Cottages	7 E6	Sanson Close

Grove Gardens South 7 E9
Grove Gardens 7 E8
Halidon Terrace 4 C3
Hallowstell View 7 G8
Harcar Court 6 D9
Hatters Lane 5 F5
Hawthorne Crescent 7 E9
Henderson Court 7 F7
Hide Hill 7 F6
High Cottages 7 H9
High Greens 5 F5
Highcliffe 7 G9
Hillcrest 6 B8
Hillside Lodge 7 E9
Hillside 7 E9
Hiveacres Road 6 C9
Homebank 6 C8
Howick Terrace 7 F8
Infirmary Square 5 F5
Islestone Court 6 D9
Ivinson Road 6 D8
Ivy Place 5 F5
James Place 7 G8
Kiln Hill 7 E7
King James Court 7 F6
Knivestone Court 6 D9
Knowe Head 7 E7
Ladywell Place 7 E7
Ladywell Road 7 E7
Lamb Court 7 E10
Lees Lane 7 F7
Lees Lane 7 F7
Lindisfarne Gate 6 C9
Loaning Meadows 5 E2
Longstone View 7 G6
Lord's Mount 5 F5
Lovaine Terrace 5 F4
Love Lane 7 F6
Lovers Walk 7 F6
Low Greens 5 F5
Magdalene Drive 5 E3
Main Street (Berwick) 7 E7
Main Street (Spittal) 7 G8
Main Street (Spittal) 7 H9
Mansefield Road 6 D9
Marygate 7 F6
Meadow Dale 6 D9
Meadow Gardens 6 D9
Meadow Grange 5 E3
Meadow Hilt 4 C3
Meadow Rigg 6 C9
Meadowlands 6 C9
Meadows, The 5 E3
Meeting House Lane (2) 7 G8
Megstone Court 6 D9
Middle Street 7 G8
Mill Strand 7 E7
Millfield Place 6 B8
Mordington Avenue 6 D9

Mount Road 7 F7
Ner Cottages 7 E6
Ness Street 7 G6
New Road 7 F6
Newfields 5 E2
North Greenwich Road 7 H8
North Road 5 E3
Northumberland Avenue 5 F4
Northumberland Road 7 F8
Oil Mill Lane (9) 7 F6
Ord Drive 7 E6
Ord Road 6 C8
Osborne Cottages 6 C8
Osborne Crescent 7 E6
Osborne Place 7 E7
Osborne Road 7 E7
Oval, The 7 E8
Palace Green 7 F6
Palace Street East 7 F6
Palace Street 7 F6
Parade School 5 F5
Parade 5 G5
Parkside 7 E8
Pastures, The 6 D8
Paxton Road 4 B5
Percy Terrace 5 F4
Pier Road 7 G6
Prince Edward Road 7 E6
Princes Opens (1) 7 G8
Princes Street 7 G8
Prior Road 7 E9
Prior View 7 E9
Promenade 7 H9
Pudding Lane 7 E6
Quay Walls 7 F6
Railway Cottages 6 B9
Railway Street 5 E5
Ravensdowne 7 G6
River Dene 7 E6
Riverside Road 7 E6
Riverview Park 7 G8
Roberts Lodge 7 E10
Roddam Court 6 D9
Rotary Way 6 B8
Rowntree Avenue 7 F8
St Aidan's Road 5 E3
St Andrews Place (2) 5 F5
St Andrew's Road 5 E3
St Bartholomew's Crescent 7 G8
St Cuthbert's Road 5 E3
St George's Road 5 E3
St Helen's Terrace 7 H8
St Katherine's Place 6 B9
St Mary's Place (1) 5 F5
Sally Port 7 F6
Sandgate 7 F6

Sandstell Road 7 G8
Sanson Close 6 D9
School Lane 7 G8
Scott's Place 5 F5
Sea Road 7 H8
Sea View 5 F3
Seafield Place 7 H9
Shielfield Terrace 7 E8
Sidey Court 5 F5
Silver Street 7 F6
South Greenwich Road 7 H9
Spittal Hall Place 7 G8
Spittal Hall Road 7 G8
Springdale 7 E9
Springfield Park 6 C9
Springhill Lane 7 E10
Stanley Close 6 C9
Stephenson Court 7 E10
Stott Court 7 E10
Summerhill Terrace 5 E4
Sunnyside Crescent 7 F8
Sunnyside Cut 7 F9
Sunnyside Mews 7 F9
Temperance Terrace 5 F5
Thornton Gate 6 C8
Tower Road 7 F7
Turret Gardens 7 E8
Tweed Close 6 C8
Tweed Street 5 F5
Union Brae 7 E6
Union Park Road 7 E6
Valley View 7 E9
Violet Terrace 5 F5
Walkergate 5 F5
Wallace Green 5 F5
Warkworth Terrace 5 F4
Waterloo Place 7 G8
Waugh Square (6) 7 F6
Weddels Court (6) 7 F6
Weddels Lane (5) 7 F6
Well Close 5 F5
Well Road 7 F7
Well Square 7 F7
Well Square 7 F7
Wellington Terrace 7 F6
West End Road 7 E6
West End 7 E6
West Street (Berwick) 7 F6
West Street (Spittal) 7 G8
Westend Court 7 E6
Westend Place 7 E6
Westfield Avenue 5 F4
Westfield Road 5 E4
Whiteadder Close 6 D9
Whitesand Close 6 D9
Windsor Crescent 5 E4
Woolmarket Mews 7 F6
Woolmarket 7 F6
Yard Heads 7 E6
Yarrow Close 6 D8

Abbots Place 18 F6
Abbotsferry Road 19 J7
Abbotsford Court 17 E5
Abbotsford Place 18 F6
Abbotsford Road 17 F5
Abbotsford Road 18 G8
Abbotsford Terrace 18 F6
Abbotslea 19 J7
Abbotsview Court 18 H7
Abbotsview Drive 18 H7
Abbotsview Gardens 18 H7
Abbotsview Lane 18 H7
Albert Place 17 E5
Anfield Gardens 18 F6
Aster Court 19 J5
Balmoral Avenue 16 C5
Balmoral Drive 16 C5
Balmoral Place 16 D4
Balmoral Road 16 C5
Balmoral Terrace 16 C5
Balnakiel Terrace 16 B2
Bank Close (4) 17 E4
Bank Court (3) 17 E4
Bank Street 17 E4
Bank Street Brae (1) 17 E4
Barr Road 17 E5
Beech Avenue 17 H5
Beechbank Place 17 E4
Blakehope Court 19 K7
Bluebell Lane 19 J5
Blynlee Lane 16 B2
Boleside Road 18 H8
Bow Butts (8) 17 E5
Bow Butts Close (9) 17 E5
Bridge Place 16 D4
Bridge Street 17 E4
Bridgend Cottages 19 L6
Brier Lane 19 J5
Broadlee Bank 19 K7
Broom Drive 19 J5
Buckholm Mill Brae 16 C2
Carlin Court 19 K7
Catrail Road 16 C3
Cemetery Road 18 G6
Channel Street 17 E4
Chapel Street 17 E4
Cherry Park 19 L7
Church Bank 17 E5
Church Square (7) 17 E5
Church Street 17 E5
Cochrane Place 18 F6
Coopersknowe Crescent 19 K5
Cornhill Court (1) 17 E5
Cornmill Square 17 E5
Cotgreen Road 19 K7
Craigpark Gardens 17 E5
Craw Wood 19 L7
Croft Street 17 F5

Dale Street	18 G6	High Buckholmside	16 D3	Meigle View	16 C4	Union Street	16 D4
Dean Street	16 C4	High Road	17 E3	Melrose Road	17 F4	Victoria Street	16 D4
Douglas Bridge	17 E4	High Street	16 D4	Melrose Road	19 J5	Waitknowe Terrace	18 G6
Douglas Place	18 F6	Hill Street	17 F5	Mill Park	16 B2	Waverley Place	18 G6
Douglas Street	17 F5	Hillside Drive	16 B1	Mossilee Crescent	16 C4	Westwood Gardens	16 B2
Duke Street	16 C3	Hollybush Road	16 D5	Mossilee Road	16 C4	Wheatlands Road	16 B2
Easter Cottages	19 K5	Honeylees Drive	19 K7	Neidpath Court	19 K6	Whin Court	19 J5
Eildon Lodge	19 K5	Huddersfield Street	17 F5	Nether Road	18 H6	Wilder Place	16 D3
Gardens		Ida Hayward	18 G6	Netherbank	18 G7	Wilderhaugh Street	16 D3
Eildon Street	16 C4	Cottage Homes (1)		Netherview	18 H7	William Law Gardens	16 A1
Ellwyn Crescent	17 F4	Island Street	16 D3	Netherdale Brae	18 G6	Windyknowe Road	16 C3
Ellwyn Terrace	17 F4	Johnstons Close	17 E4	Oatlands Terrace	18 F6	Winston Place	19 J6
Elm Grove	17 E5	Jura Drive	19 L7	Overhaugh Street	17 E4	Winston Road	19 J5
Elm Row	17 E5	Kenilworth Avenue	18 H6	Park Street	17 E4	Wood Street	16 B2
Essenside Drive	19 K6	Killie Croft	19 L7	Parsonage Road	18 F6	Woodlee	16 B2
Essenside Place	19 K6	Killie Court	19 K7	Paterson Street	18 F6	Woodside Drive	16 C3
Forebrae Park	17 E4	Kilknowe Place	16 B3	Paton Street	17 E5	Woodside Place	16 C2
Forest Avenue	16 D5	King Street	16 C3	Plumtree Place	16 C3	Woodstock Avenue	18 H6
Forest Crescent	16 C5	Kings Knowe Village	18 G6	Plumtreehall Brae	16 C2	Woodstock Road	18 H6
Forest Gardens	16 C4	Kingsknowe Drive	18 H7	Primrose Bank	19 J5	Wylies Brae	17 F4
Forest Hill	16 C4	Kingsknowe Gardens	18 H7	Princes Street	16 D3		
Forest Place	16 C5	Kingsknowe Place	18 H7	Pringle Lane	16 B2		
Forest Road	16 D5	Kingsknowes	18 H7	Queen Street	16 C3		
Gala Lane	17 E4	Cottages		Riverside Drive	19 J7		
Gala Park	16 D4	Kirkbrae	16 D4	Roberts Court	17 E3		
Gala Park	17 E4	Ladhope Bank	16 D3	Roberts Grove	17 E3		
Gardens (5)		Ladhope Crescent	17 E3	Roger Quin Gardens	18 G7		
Gala Park Place	16 D4	Ladhope Drive	17 E3	Rose Court	17 H5		
Gala Park Road	17 E4	Ladhope Vale	17 E4	Rosebank Place	16 D4		
Gala Terrace	17 E5	Lady Moss	19 J7	Roxburgh House	16 D4		
Galabank Street	17 F5	Langhaugh Crescent	17 F5	Court			
Galafoot Lane	19 J6	Langhaugh Gardens	17 F5	Roxburgh Place	16 D4		
Galafoot Road	19 J7	Langhaugh Lane	17 F5	Roxburgh Street	16 D4		
Galahill Crescent	18 E6	Langlee Avenue	18 H6	Sanderson Court	16 D3		
Gibson's Close (2)	17 E4	Langlee Drive	17 H5	Scott Crescent	17 E5		
Gill's Close	17 E4	Langlee Road	18 H6	Scott Street	16 D4		
Glebe Place	17 E5	Larch Grove	17 H5	Shielwood Court	19 K7		
Glendinning Terrace	16 D2	Larchbank Street	18 G6	Sime Place	17 E4		
Glenfield Avenue	17 G5	Larkspur Court	19 J5	St Andrew Street	16 D4		
Glenfield Court	17 F5	Laurel Grove	17 H5	St John Street	17 E5		
Glenfield Crescent	17 G5	Lawyers Brae	17 E5	Stanley Street	16 D4		
Glenfield Road West	17 F5	Lee Brae	16 C2	Station Brae	17 E4		
Glenfield Road East	17 G5	Lintburn Place	16 D4	Stirling Place	17 E4		
Glenfield Terrace	17 G5	Lintburn Street	16 D4	Stirling Street	17 E4		
Gorse Lane	19 J5	Livingstone Place	16 D5	Stobshaw Place	19 K6		
Green Street	17 E4	Lochend	19 K7	Stobshaw Terrace	19 K6		
Greenbank Street	17 F5	Low Buckholmside	16 D3	Talisman Avenue	17 H5		
Gun Knowe Bank	19 K7	Lowood Park	19 J7	Tea Street	17 E5		
Haining Drive	19 K6	Lucy Sanderson	18 G6	Thistle Street	16 D4		
Hall Place	16 D4	Cottage Homes (2)		Thornbank Street	17 F5		
Hall Street	16 D4	Magdala Terrace	16 C2	Torwoodlee Road	16 B2		
Halliburton Place	16 C2	Manse Lane	16 C3	Tulley Court	17 F5		
Halliburton Terrace	16 D3	Manse Place	16 C3	Tweed Crescent	18 G6		
Hareshaw Bank	19 K7	Manse Street	16 C3	Tweed Grove	18 G6		
Hawthorn Road	17 H5	Marigold Bank	17 H5	Tweed Road	18 G7		
Hayward Drive	18 F6	Marigold Drive	19 J5	Tweed Road	18 H6		
Hazeldean	16 D4	Market Street	17 E4	Tweed Terrace	18 G6		
Heather Court	19 J5	Maryfield Gardens	16 D3	Tweedbank Avenue	19 L7		
Heatheryett Drive	17 E3	Meigle Street	16 C4	Tweedbank Drive	19 K8		
Heathery Rig	19 J7			Tweedbank View	19 L7		